EXPERIENCING GOD

Other books by Michael Eaton:

In the same series as this book:

Living A Godly Life
Enjoying God's Worldwide Church

Forthcoming
Applying God's Law

Ecclesiastes (Tyndale Commentary) – IVP
The Baptism with the Spirit – IVP
Living Under Grace (Romans 6–7)
A Theology of Encouragement – Paternoster

THEOLOGY FOR BEGINNERS

EXPERIENCING GOD

by
Michael Eaton

OM
publishing

Copyright © 1998 Michael Eaton

First published in 1998 by OM Publishing

04 03 02 01 00 99 98   7 6 5 4 3 2 1

OM Publishing is an imprint of Paternoster Publishing,
PO Box 300, Carlisle, Cumbria, CA3 0QS, UK
http://www.paternoster-publishing.com

The right of Michael Eaton to be identified as the Author of this
Work has been asserted by him in accordance with the Copyright,
Designs and Patents Act 1988.

British Library Cataloguing in Publication Data
A catalogue record for this book is available from the British Library

ISBN 1-85078-308-X

Cover Design by Forum Marketing, Newcastle upon Tyne
Typeset by WestKey Ltd, Falmouth, Cornwall
Printed in Great Britain by
Caledonian International Book Manufacturing Ltd, Glasgow

Contents

Preface

Like *Living A Godly Life* and *Enjoying the Worldwide Church*, this book is a simple exposition of a part of Christian doctrine, this time the doctrine of God. All of these books are summaries of what I have been preaching. Every chapter is a summary of one, two or several 'messages' that have been preached. I have no interest in Christian doctrine unless it can change the lives of ordinary people. Local applications that were in the original preaching have been omitted. Preachers have to do their local application of the message as they go along without necessarily putting it in printed versions. I do not include here remarks that I make in my preaching that refer to events that happened on the streets of Nairobi or that were mentioned in yesterday's newspaper or wherever. Yet such remarks might well have come in the originals of these chapters; but these pages are intended to be less locally applied and therefore of wider interest.

I am restating Christian doctrine in a simple way for Christians interested in the teaching of God's Word. Logically this is the first in the series.

The whole list is as follows:

3. Experiencing God
   Honouring God's Creation
   Understanding Yourself
   Glorifying Jesus Christ
   Appreciating Salvation
   Experiencing the Holy Spirit
1. Living A Godly Life
   Listening to God

4. Applying God's Law
    Enjoying God's Church Worldwide
    Preparing for the Future

In most cases it takes more than one little book for me to cover the topic. *Enjoying God's Church* added the word 'Worldwide' and covered half of what I wanted to say. A book on the local church is yet to come. Similarly this little book will have a successor in which I shall have things to say about other characteristics of God, his love, his mercy and compassion, and so on.

Preaching and writing about knowing God is tricky. There is a difference between knowing God and knowing *about* God. It is good to know about God but we are talking about something greater and higher. The people who crucified Jesus knew a lot *about* God but they did not know God. Sometimes people preach or write about knowing God, when really what they are talking or writing on is knowing *about* God. Whether I have done any better is for others to decide. The book on the subject that I enjoy most is A.W. Tozer's *The Pursuit of God* but it is quite different from (say) J.I. Packer's *Knowing God*. Actually Packer's title fits Tozer's book better than his own which could be called *The Attributes of God* – but then that is the title of a book by A.W. Pink! I am trying to speak and write about both knowing about God and knowing God. Knowing God includes knowing about him, but it is a matter of learning about him in a practical and experiential way. I could do with a little of A.W. Tozer's anointing!

Although I try to write in a simple, down-to-earth manner, I emphasize that this is book of Christian doctrine. It does not have many stories or illustrations. Such material is mostly omitted. It is simple theology, written for ordinary people.

As I have explained before, all translations are my own.

As well as books just mentioned, others have meant a lot to me over the years, H. Bavinck's *Doctrine of God*, A.W. Pink's *Attributes of God* and *Sovereignty of God* – although the latter is too harsh for my liking. The Puritan, Stephen Charnock, wrote *The Existence and Attributes of God*, and J.W. Wenham's *The Goodness of God* addresses a particular problem. Adrio König's *Here Am I* has many fresh insights and is valuable. I have profited from J.E. Frame's *The Doctrine of the Knowledge of God*. I acknowledge the influence of all of these works in my own preaching which is presented here. Another which could be mentioned is D.G. Bloesch, *God the Almighty* (Paternoster, 1995), but I had not read it at the time I was preaching on these topics. Evangelical theologians – if they ever glance at such a simple book as this – will also notice the influence of Francis Schaeffer and Cornelius Van Til.

As always I am grateful for the encouragement of my family and friends, many of whom help check my manuscripts for simplicity. Though I do not always heed their every word their love and affection means much to me. The people of Chrisco Fellowship, Nairobi, heard many of the chapters of this book in lunchtime services. They are precious people.

Michael Eaton
Nairobi

PART ONE:
THE EXISTENCE OF GOD

ONE

Knowing that God is Real

It is possible to know God. To some extent everyone knows God already. 'Although they knew God', says the Bible, 'they did not glorify him as God and they did not give thanks to him'. People rebel against God despite what they know. The very world around us and the fact of our existence gives everyone a knowledge of God. Yet although God is known, men and women do not generally glorify him as God, and they do not give thanks to him.

But we need to know God in a much deeper way than that. Although in one sense everyone knows God, in another sense we are ignorant of him and need to get to know God. There is a deeper, richer, livelier knowledge of God to be had than the knowledge that we are born with. In a deeper sense only those who know Jesus know God. Jesus said: 'This is eternal life, that they may know you, the only true God, and Jesus Christ whom you have sent'.

It is not just information about God that we need. We need to know God himself. We need to know God through Jesus, which is the only way to know him. Then we need to have a greater hunger and thirst for God. We need to be like the psalmist who said, 'My soul thirsts for God, for the living God'.

I believe that you already know that God exists. The Bible says that everyone has a sense that God is there. No doubt there are some sincere atheists, although no one is born an atheist. Atheism is not natural; it is a matter of indoctrination. Everyone is born conscious that God is there.

Before we come to salvation, we suppress the knowledge of God that we are born with. But I am assuming that you know that God exists or at least that you are willing to pray 'God – if you are there – please reveal yourself to me'. Personally since as far back as I can remember I never had any doubts that God existed. Maybe I got it from my parents. They were not church-going people and they certainly never talked to me about Jesus, but when a relative of mine declared he was an atheist they were shocked and horrified! They took it for granted that God exists but had no interest in God for the practical purposes of their day-to-day living. That is the way I grew up as a child. But we were not atheists! Many people are like that. They do not care about religion or church but they know that God exists.

But maybe – I don't know – atheists can have more of a problem than I am capable of appreciating. All I can say is that I personally am one hundred per cent sure that God exists, and that the Christian gospel is true. It is this Christian gospel I want to explain and elaborate, and, as I say, I am taking it that you already know God exists or that you are willing to pray, 'God – if you are there – please reveal yourself to me'.

I suppose there are about five major problems about God that give some encouragement to people who wish to be atheists. There is (i) the fact of evil, (ii) the question whether it is necessary to hold to the idea of God in order to explain the world, (iii) the disheartening experience we may have had of boring and super-stitious traditional religion, (iv) the thought that since there are many religions and they cannot all be right so probably they are all the same or none of them is right, and (v) there are some philosophical ideas around that are used to argue against God, or against religious language.

I shall say something about all of these five difficulties later, but for the moment I am simply taking it for granted that you know God exists.

But do you really want to know God? It is not only intellectual problems that get in the way when it comes to knowing God. There are intellectual problems for Christians, and there are intellectual problems for atheists and agnostics too! Everyone lives by his or her own set of assumptions about life that cannot be proved by anyone!

The real question is not intellectual. It has to do with our willingness to have Someone greater than us who might tell us what to do and how to live! How do you feel when, as you approach God, you realize more of your own sinfulness? Maybe at the moment you hardly bother thinking about sin. You live more or less as you like, and you don't want any God to interfere! Many people back away from God, simply because they know that God is likely to talk to them about their sins. They fear that their sins will have to be dealt with. But what if you do not need to have this fear? What if God will only mention your sins in order to forgive them? What if the life that God would like to bring you into is more enjoyable than the kind of doing-what-I-like thing that you are in at the moment?

Sin is a great barrier to knowing God. Strangely, so is religion! I can think of nothing that discourages the real knowledge of God as religion or (as I prefer to call it) religiosity. Scandalous sin is bad enough but self-righteous religiosity is worse! Jesus said he did not have anything to say to the righteous! Well, all these things will have to be dealt with, but for the moment I simply want to assume that God exists and start talking about him. We'll come back to the questions afterwards. After all, there is no value talking about God if we do not know what we mean when we use the word God. I am not planning to start 'proving' God by some kind of scientific method. The reality of God has to be known in another way than that! Even if you have not come to experience salvation you have a feeling in your heart that God exists.

This is the point made by a famous passage in the Bible, Romans 1:18–32. It talks about the things that happen to any society that tries to deny that God exists.

It is a basic fact of life that everyone rejects the love of God shown in creation. This makes God angry. Everyone everywhere knows that God exists, and they know that God is good to them. Yet by nature, by the way we are born, we reject the feeling we have that God is there. By nature we do not respond to him.

I assume you have a Bible. Try reading Romans 1:18–32. It says that God is angry with sin (1:18a) and that people sin wilfully despite what they know (1:18b). In 1:19–21a the point is developed and Paul deals with the sinfulness of resisting God. There are four points in what he says: (i) God is known (Rom. 1:19a), (ii) God has given a revelation, a self-disclosure, so that everyone knows him (Rom. 1:19b); (iii) creation gives everyone this knowledge of God (Rom. 1:20); (iv) although God is known, men and women do not generally glorify him (Rom. 1:21a).

Then Paul goes on to deal with the consequences of man's rejection of God. There are five stages in the outworking of God's wrath (Rom. 1:21b–32). Stage one is the darkening of the mind (Rom. 1:21b). Because men and women suppress their instinctive knowledge of God the result is that the mind is unable to think straight with regard to the things of God. Stage two is false religion (Rom. 1:22–23). Those who do not worship God worship weird and ugly substitutes. Stage three is uncontrolled desires (Rom. 1:24–25). Sexual impurity begins to take over. Stage four is unnatural sin (Rom. 1:26–27). Some kinds of sexual sin are at least natural, but as the society declines even further unnatural sin begins to come in. Stage five is the fulness of sin (Rom. 1:28–32). Sin runs wild. This is the end of the road. When a society reaches such depths the end of that culture is at hand. Only God's mercy can prevent utter ruin.

TWO

Arguing God's Existence

The reason why the good news about Jesus is so indispensable is that God is angry about the sin of suppressing what is known about him. 'The wrath of God is revealed from heaven against all ungodliness and unrighteousness of people who hold down the truth in unrighteousness'.

God is there. God is also close to us. The Bible says we should 'feel after' him (Acts 17:27). God, says the Bible, is lord of heaven and earth. He is the one who sustains life and arranges our existence (Acts 17:24b–25). He orders the human race (Acts 24:26) and determines where the nations have their particular dwelling-places on earth (Acts 24:26b). God reveals himself in nature, in his rule of the world, in the circumstances of our lives. He does this so that we shall 'feel after' him or 'grope after' him, says the Bible (Acts 17:27). God is not very far away. Even pagan Greeks were expected to feel after him. With the much clearer revelation we now have about Jesus, God is nearer than ever. He is able to be found.

This is how we approach God's existence. We *know* God is there. We must feel out for him. He is there. It is possible to contact him. We need to know God in a personal way. The Athenians of Acts 17 did not have much to help them. We have much fuller help now, in the Bible, and in the help of people who have found God personally through Jesus Christ. And, as I have said, it is not just information about God that we need. We need to know God himself.

It will involve repentance, recognizing our wrong doing and accepting God's hatred of it. It will involve us in trusting Jesus, God's Saviour. This is the way to know God himself.

It might be asked, 'Is it possible to prove God's existence?' Various proofs for God's existence have been suggested by philosophers, but it is a mistake to make much use of them. Yet it may be of interest to know about them, and they have a certain appeal, although in terms of strict logic they are without any value.

There is the argument from cause (the 'cosmological' argument). This was first urged by the Greek philosopher Aristotle and then was used by Thomas Aquinas. The idea is that there has to be an Un-Moved Mover, an Un-Caused-Cause, behind this world.

There is the argument from design (the 'teleological' argument). Sometimes it has been put to us in an old illustration (which goes back to William Paley). The illustration goes like this. Imagine that you were on a deserted island – in the days when there were deserted islands! – where perhaps no one had ever been before. Then you discover a watch on the island. You look at the watch. Obviously it is not a stone or a plant or a piece of rock. Obviously it has design and purpose. The evidence of design in the watch would prove someone had been on the deserted island. The evidence of design would prove that a maker was behind the watch. So it is with this universe. Its obvious design is proof of a designer.

Then, thirdly, there is the argument from conscience (the 'anthropological' argument). We all have a sense of responsibility. This implies that there is a judge over this world.

A fourth argument is the argument from the nature of existence, or from the nature of our thinking (the 'ontological' argument). We have the idea of a perfect being. But existence is part of perfection. It is difficult to conceive of a perfect being who does not exist!

Actually all of these arguments are weak! If taken with strict logic, there are serious objections to them. (The same thing is true of atheists' arguments. Their logic is weak too!) The objections to these traditional Christian arguments are as follows: (i) These arguments tend to contradict themselves. The idea that 'Everything must have a cause' is used to prove God who has no cause! (ii) The kind of God who is proved in this way is not the God of the Bible. (iii) There is the problem of the unity of everything that you 'prove'. Does the first designer have to be the same as the first causer? Logically why could there not be a multiplicity of gods? (iv) With all these arguments the fact that we have an idea about a certain god does not prove that the reality exists. It is impossible to deduce reality from the nature of thought.

Actually nothing can prove God because God is the proof of everything else! One cannot get to anything behind God with which to prove him. The best approach to proof is simply to assume God – as the Bible does. The God of the Bible is necessary for the existence of everything else. God is the explanation of everything else that exists. Presupposition is the best proof. The fact that the world is as it is requires the God of the Bible. The question is: what is it that, when presupposed, explains everything else?

Some Christians, especially Roman Catholics, have tended to try to use a kind of 'neutral' human reasoning to argue their way to God. They act as if reason comes first, and God's revelation supplements reason. But the opposite is true. Revelation is first. Reason supplements revelation. As Anselm put it in the eleventh century, we do not understand in order to believe, but we believe in order to understand.

There is a very different kind of argument for God and that is the argument from what God has done in history. God has acted in the history of the world. The Old Testament contains the prophecies and predictions of what he would do. Then it contains the records of what he did. There is the amazing life of Jesus, and his claims to be the Son of God. There is his resurrection from the dead and the outpouring of the Holy Spirit a few weeks later. There is the story of the endless revivals in the Christian church. The church has great power and life. True Christians are alive with the power of God! But then the church tends to become dead and traditional. Just when you think the dead and decadent church is going to die out altogether, God revives it and a new powerful movement of the Christian faith starts somewhere (often leaving the traditional Christians aside!) These things are so amazing that they demand explanation. The explanation is God and his mighty acts! The story of dead traditional Christianity is a bit boring. The story of revivals is one of the greatest proofs that there can be of the reality of God.

The biblical approach to the existence of God is not philosophical at all. The Bible assumes and asserts that God exists, not that 'a god' exists but that the God and Father of our Lord Jesus Christ exists. The Bible simply takes God's existence for granted. Its opening sentence assumes God is real: 'In the beginning God . . .' (Gen. 1:1). It does not try to prove anything. Romans 1:19–21 says (in effect): 'You know God is there, don't you?' The wrath of God is revealed because men and women suppress what they know. God has made it plain. Everyone has this consciousness. In the Bible there is no discussion of this question at all. There is just sheer assertion without argument. The Bible claims that the person who denies God is a 'fool'. He has moral reasons for denying what he senses to be true. No one is naturally an atheist. No one is born an atheist. The fool says in his heart, 'No God!' (Ps. 14:1). When you talk to an atheist he or she is not neutral. He or she has to suppress something. No one is surprised to discover God exists.

However this knowledge of God is not an intimate or saving knowledge. The kind of knowledge that God wants is more practical. It is faith-knowledge. We cannot please God by a detached knowledge. We please God by relying on him practically. We must practically live on him in his service. Without faith it is impossible to please God. And faith is not believing that God exists. It is taking God at his word. It is building one's entire life on what he says to us.

When we talk to an atheist – and there are not many of them around – we have to look to the Holy Spirit to work in his or her heart. Just arguing will do no good at all. But we must remember John 7:17. Jesus said: 'If anyone is willing to do God's will, he shall know about this teaching and will know whether it comes from God or whether I am speaking of myself'. The question for an atheist is: 'If the God of the Bible does exist are you ready to have him deal with you?' If such a God exists would he not be capable of revealing himself to you? He is there. You already have an inner sense that God is there. Reach out for him. Be honest with him. Talk to him. Approach him. Come to him in the name of Jesus. He will reveal himself in a yet deeper way. You will get to know him personally.

THREE

An Excuse for Atheists:
Religious Tyranny

Let me come back to this matter of atheism once again. This book is about knowing God. I would like everyone to know God in the way I believe truly 'saved' people know him, and in the way in which I have found God myself. But I can appreciate that many atheists have some good excuses for not identifying with the Christian faith and – although I think that deep down they know that God is real – I have some sympathy with some of their excuses!

Anyone who reads the newspaper must surely find at least one good excuse for disliking religion and denying God. If I were not a Christian, and if I did not know God for myself, I think the biggest reason why I would dislike the idea of God is the religious tyrannies that go on in different parts of the world. One thinks of a host of religious wars past and present: the Crusades of medieval Europe, the persecution of Jews, the persecution of one section of Christendom by another section of Christendom, Catholics and Protestants in Northern Ireland, the Muslim persecution of Christians in southern Sudan, the current rise in aggression among certain Hindus to the point of wanting non-Hindu Indians to be denied citizenship in India. It is enough to drive anyone into a dislike of anything even vaguely religious. Many secular people feel that the Christian faith has to be left aside because all expressions of religious faith must be left aside – because they cause so much trouble!

To this, two things must be said: atheism, agnosticism and secularism have as much potential to be persecuting powers as any religious faith. It is certainly no solution to the problem to replace religious persecution with secular persecution! Russia's old-style atheist regime was as vicious as a persecuting agency as the worst forms of religious inquisition. Spokesmen for secularism wish in their own way to discriminate against any kind of religious faith. Theirs too is a persecuting faith!

The second point is: the Christian faith at its best has been the pioneer of religious toleration.

The real answer to this problem is the separation of ideology and state power. Every state needs to uphold rights for minorities. But it must be remembered that the greatest foundation of religious toleration has been Jesus' teaching about the state. No one has an unblemished record in this matter, but the greatest defenders of freedom so far have been countries whose origins are Christian. I have already dealt with this matter of church and state in another book[1], and I hardly want to write the same thing twice! But it was Jesus who said, 'Render to Caesar the things that are Caesar's and to God the things that are God's'. In saying this he was talking of religious ideology and state-power as two entities, not one, and was urging us to relate to them distinctly. For most people of Jesus' day, either Caesar had all power and could be dictatorial about religion, or God had all power and could dictate about Caesar! The latter is true enough! But such a truth is not to be made the basis of political power, and faith must not come by state coercion.

It was the fact that all nations had state religions that made the question 'Shall we pay taxes to Caesar?' such a dangerous question for Jesus. Jesus did something startlingly innovative in separating out two realms; it was unique and unprecedented in the history of the world.

The Christian view of society – although there is insufficient agreement among Christians concerning the matter – is that a plurality of faiths and ideologies must be allowed in each country. This means that a religious establishment must not be imposed; and neither must a secular establishment be imposed! Governments need to be less ambitious altogether in the matter of imposing ideologies.

Perhaps it will be said, 'Neutrality is impossible; a government has to impose some kind of ideology'. Yes, it is true that neutrality is impossible, but politics works by consensus. Politics by coercion is not the answer. It is surely necessary that whatever might be the majority ideology in a country, that country should allow tolerance of other viewpoints. People should surely be allowed to think and to come to their own conclusions. When people come to different convictions and conclusions about the nature of life and of ethical standards, no doubt it will create problems in working together at a national level. But this problem cannot be abolished by genocidal extermination of other viewpoints. 'Christian' countries, so-called, allow freedom for Muslims (to take one example). Muslims are quite free to practise their faith when they come to countries with a traditionally Christian background – USA, Britain, and elsewhere. Christian ideals have promoted toleration. Muslim countries should accordingly do the same thing when the situation is the other way around. They should allow freedom for Christians – but where they have power they do not.

The real issue at this point is not whether there is a god or not. It is not a matter of which religion is right, if any. It is a matter of how does ideology or religion or political party relate to minorities and to varied religious viewpoints. One can understand people becoming atheists because of dislike of various kinds of fundamentalism, Hindu fundamentalism or Islamic fundamentalism or whatever. But secular fundamentalism is just as bad! The answer is surely to insist on politics by as-good-a-consensus-as-one-can-get, not politics-by-imposed-religion whether it be Hinduism or Islam or Catholicism or faith in secularism. Historically this view of the separation-of-church-and-state has arisen from the Bible by radically-minded Christians. Roger Williams – a radical Bible-believing Christian – was the founder of religious toleration in America. The Levellers – a group of Bible-believing Christians in Oliver Cromwell's army – were the founders of religious toleration in Britain. A radically biblical view of plurality of ideologies within each state is the greatest protection of toleration. Faith must be a matter of free choice. Freedom includes freedom for all minorities whether religious minorities or secular minorities. Political leadership by as-good-a-consensus-as-one-can-get is a necessary foundation for toleration. These are the remedies for this particular problem that troubles secular man. And it is a radical biblical faith – and I think that alone – which will uphold such freedom.

It may seem strange that such matters are mentioned in a book about the doctrine of God. Is this book about God or about politics? Well, it is about God! But religious tyrannies in the world are the greatest argument for atheism. In the same way atheist tyrannies that have been witnessed in the twentieth century are a great argument in favour of the biblical view of God – a God who wishes to be loved by means of voluntary faith, not by means of state coercion.

Many countries of the world are the object of vigorous Muslim 'evangelism'. Christians also can be energetic mission-aries. Hinduism, despite its reputation for tolerance, is increas-ingly wishing to have a monopoly in India – and even elsewhere. The whole world must accept the faith of India – they say! The question to be asked is: what will a country be like if any of these ideologies get their way? What will a country be like if Muslim Sheria law is imposed? Ask the southern Sudanese! What will India be like if Hindu fundamentalism gets its way? What will it be like if Catholicism becomes a state religion in this part of the world or that part of the world? Consider the Crusades!

And then ask the opposite question: what would happen if the biblical view of ideological freedom were upheld? And so on.

There are other reasons why people become atheists. I shall have something to say about them as we proceed. But to the average secular-minded man or woman bothered by religious tyranny it can be said quite simply: the answer to tyranny of this kind is the biblical view of ideological plurality. The atheist himself would also be a tyrant if he were given a chance. Nothing will preserve our freedoms except to have some reason for maintaining genuine ideological plurality. Most people who say they want plurality actually want an imposed politically correct relativism in which nothing is meant to be true for certain. It is this relativism which is imposed with a tyranny as bad as any other – and such a tyrant thinks he is upholding freedom! The only pluralism which will truly preserve liberty is the biblical view of ideological plurality. To allow a society with groups holding different and deeply held religious convictions, each of which are in some sense making exclusive claims, might be difficult. But plurality is not plurality unless it is achieved.

'Render to Caesar the things that are Caesar's' – no matter who Caesar might be and what his religion might be. But 'render to God the things that are God's' – and that will involve ideological plurality, for Caesar's faith might not be ours.

Endnote

1. See ch. 5 'Church and State' in Eaton, M. *Enjoying the Worldwide Church*

FOUR

Is God Beyond Our Ability to know Him?

There is another form of rejection of the God and Father of our Lord Jesus Christ that goes like this: since there are many religions that all claim to be pathways to God it would be bigotry to regard only one as right. We must view them all as being, in different ways, roads to God.

This leads into a kind of practical atheism. If all religions are roughly the same in being pathways to God, then nothing distinctive is known about God and we may as well live without him. 'Maybe there's a god' – says this particular line of thought – 'but no one religion is the right one. All religions are worshipping the same God. There are just different ideas about him and different routes to get to him'.

There is something strangely superficial about this line of thought. It is trying to say, 'Maybe all religions are equally right and as good as each other' but if this line of thought is right, it really means that all religions are wrong in what they actually say, and are as bad as each other!

If all religions are equal, Jesus was drastically and disastrously wrong when he said, 'No man comes to the Father except by me'.

If all religions are equal, Muslims are drastically and disastrously wrong when they say the Qur'an and it alone is the inerrantly inspired, untranslatably perfect, Scriptures from God.

If all religions are right Hindus are wrong if they (for example) portray Krishna as the incarnation of the god Vishnu, or the god Shiva as the paradoxical combination of asceticism and eroticism.

All religions are right somehow turns out to mean all religions are wrong!

The idea that some people have is that Old Testament prophets, Zoroaster, Confucius, Gautama the Buddha, the writers of the Bhagavad Gita, Socrates, Plato, Jesus, Mohammed, the apostle Paul, Mahatma Gandhi, are all somehow great prophets of God and bear witness to the reality of God. There is just one great God and all these figures are somehow pointing to him.

Well, it is a nice idea, but anyone with the slightest knowledge of this list – the Old Testament prophets, Zoroaster, Confucius, Gautama and so on – knows that many of these people present utterly contradictory ideas. The idea that they are somehow all witnessing to the same divine reality is fine – as long as you never read any of them! The Old Testament prophets, Jesus and Paul were certainly giving compatible teachings. They all say that God intended that all nations should be blessed through a descendant of Abraham, and that God stepped into history with a revelation that created one nation, Israel, and sent a Messiah within that one nation to be the one and only way of salvation for the world. The Old Testament prophets, Jesus and Paul are in the same line of succession; the later teaching is a development of the earlier. There is no problem about putting those three in a list.

But the longer list above is a mixed bag, and the Jesus of the Bible is not one among many others! The trouble with this list is that these different prophets – Zoroaster, Confucius, Gautama and so on – give teaching such that, if one is right, many of the others are wrong! They certainly say things quite incompatible with Christian faith. Christians who know their Bible have to be somewhat opposed to Islam – no matter how pleasant they may wish to be to Muslim friends – because they know that the teachings of the Qur'an are different from what they believe. Muslims who know the Qur'an will always oppose Christians – no matter how friendly they might perhaps wish to be – because they know that what they are saying about Jesus and what Christians are saying about Jesus are radically and incompatibly different.

The idea that all religions are saying the same thing is only credible if you never listen to any of them! It is quite impossible to reconcile the ideas about reincarnation in Hinduism, and the ideas about heaven and hell and Jesus as the judge in the Christian faith, and the concept of a sensuous bliss for followers of Mohammed, in Islam. If one idea is right, the others are wrong. It is possible to argue that all religions are wrong. But to argue that all religions are right is the most absurd nonsense. Only by ignoring what any religion says can such a claim be made.

What this line of thought really means is that all religions are wrong – a much easier proposition to defend! Maybe what is really meant is something like this:

> I suppose it is quite likely that there is a God somewhere. But all the religions of the world are really contradictory. They are all pushing their own particular interpretations. But actually there is no reason for preferring one line of interpretation over another. The truth is they are all just feeble attempts to get to God. If one is right all the others are wrong. Probably they are all wrong. We really do not know much about God at all. He is so unimaginably remote. The best thing I can do is get on with living and enjoying myself as best as I can. For all practical purposes it is as if God did not exist. Maybe the religions have got something but they don't seem to agree. So although I believe in God I will not let religion bother me very much. I'll just get on with life as best as I can.

This sounds like a very easygoing, undemanding, tolerant sort of religion, but it has many weaknesses in it.

1. This line of thought is really saying that God is not capable of revealing himself.

2. This line of thought is arguing a definite view of God. There is a theology in it. The god of this approach is unknowable, irrelevant to life, and makes no claims upon us. He is not a judge or a king. He does not punish sin. Nothing we do really matters to him and he does not matter to us. This is a religion too but a very nonchalant one. Yet it has a view of God that is as definite and as dogmatic as any other religion! It has a specially easygoing deity! It is not neutral in its view of the other religions, since it has a god of its own!

3. This line of thought is really saying that my relationship to God does not make much difference to my future either immediately or beyond the grave.

Make no mistake. This easygoing religion has some definite ideas in it! My question is: what if these ideas are wrong?

1. What if among the competing claims about God one approach is right, and the others are wrong? Surely it is possible that this is the case. Are we so sure that no one ever has found the truth about God? This easygoing religion I have mentioned surely does not have much depth of thought in it? What if it is totally and utterly wrong? It says that all the other religions are wrong. But what if it is itself wrong? Can you be so sure it is right?

2. What if God is capable of revealing himself? The easygoing, all-religions-are-the-same religion is making an assumption. It assumes that there is no way that God will reveal himself. But what if that assumption is itself wrong? What if God is very capable of revealing himself in such a way that we can be unshakeably certain that God has revealed himself to us and has spoken to us?

3. What if this easygoing religion has an utterly wrong view of God? What if the God of the Bible is as he says he is: loving, pure, generous, sin-hating, spiritual, unified, unique, self-sufficient, personal, powerful, alive? What if God is 'the jealous God' of the Bible, the God who does not like us to worship a rival? What if the biblical picture of God's vastness, God's eternity, God's knowledge, wisdom, truthfulness, faithfulness, love, mercy, grace, patience, long-suffering, compassion, goodness, holiness, righteousness – what if this picture is true? What if God is a God who can be angry about sin? What if God is exalted, great, excellent, beautiful, glorious, happy within himself and wanting to overcome the barriers to happiness in his creatures, the men and women of planet earth?

Are we so sure that the easygoing, all-religions-are-the-same God is superior to the God of the Bible?

This line of thought that I have mentioned is arguing – in its own way – a definite view of God but what if its view of God is wrong?

What if God can be known? I am writing about how to know God. What if the God of the Bible can be known?

The various religions each lead to a certain kind of society. Which one do we want? What kind of society would I like to see? Go to India (or at least read some books!) and ask the question, 'What does Hinduism lead to?' I make no judgment about it here. I only ask: are all religions really the same?

It is possible to ask about the society that Islam produces. One can look at countries where there are both Muslims and Christians, and one can ask, 'If Christians were given their freedom, what kind of society would result? If Muslims were given freedom to impose Sheria law, what kind of society would result?' I give no answers at this point. I only ask questions, but surely they are reasonable questions.

Then one can do the same thing with different versions of the Christian faith. There is medieval catholicism and the rise of Christian Europe. There is the kind of life that arose when Christians first went to America in the 1620s and 1630s to implement as best as they could their ideas about life. What would the world be like if everyone believed in Jesus' teaching (although there is no reason to think everyone ever will!)? What would the world be like if people came to know the God of the Bible in the way that Christians claim is possible?

Also, the Christian faith makes historical claims. At the heart of the Christian view of God is our faith in something that happened in history. The gospel of Jesus is the only faith that claims that God has a Son, a one-and-only Son, and that the Son of God was born in Bethlehem, and died on a cross, and rose again from the dead, and now reigns as king of the universe. Some of these claims are claims to events in history. The Christian faith is an understanding about certain events that have appeared in the records of our planet. They can be investigated!

Also, the Christian faith makes claims about what happens when we receive the living Lord Jesus Christ into our lives. We may find some Christians who have been 'born again', and we may get them to tell us what happened when they believed that Jesus died for their sins, when they believed that Jesus is alive, when they spoke to Jesus Christ and asked him to be the Lord of their lives.

Are all religions the same? Is the God of the Bible another version of the gods of other religions? Surely not. Christians have nothing to fear from comparative religions. The more comparing that is done, the more the unique claims of the Bible will stand out. Our fear is not that people ask too many questions. Our complaint is that they ask too few questions! Let all the questions be asked – as many as possible. Christians do not have all the answers – nor does any other similar group of people. But we do believe the Christian view of God can stand any amount of examination – the more the better.

I have already given my reasons – in the previous chapter – for wanting and urging religious toleration. But this is not to claim that any idea of God is right, and that all religions are equal. Far from it. Most of them must be wrong. But perhaps God will speak to us and show us himself. This is the claim of the Christian gospel and of the Bible. If God will reveal himself to us, then there is a way of choosing between the various claims about God that are made. Indeed we are shut up to this as the only hope. There are so many man-made ideas about God. Who has the ability to choose between them? But if the God of the Bible will himself speak to me and guide me – that is another matter. But this is precisely the claim of the Bible. The God of the Bible claims to be a living God, a speaking God, a God who reveals himself in and through Jesus Christ.

FIVE

Atheism and some Basic Questions

No doubt there are sincere atheists, although as I have said I rather suspect that no one is born an atheist. I have mentioned some reasons that make atheists feel justified in their atheism – or at least that I would use to defend my position if I were an atheist!

It seems atheism has to be taught, just as the Christmas story of baby Jesus gets taught in countries which have a Christian background and the story of Mohammed gets taught in Muslim countries. One might think that someone who is not taught anything religious might be an atheist, just because he has not been taught any religion. But it does not seem to work that way. Everyone everywhere seems to believe in some kind of God. Even attempts to suppress religious faith do not have much success.

Atheism is a modern phenomenon, something that has arisen as modern scientific method came into being following 'the Enlightenment of the eighteenth century. Before the Enlightenment in Europe there was scarcely any such thing as atheism – although Christians were accused of atheism because they had no idols in their places of worship. When pagan Romans broke into early Christian buildings to see what god they worshipped they were amazed to find no idol or statue or any god at all! As a result they called Christians atheists and said they did not believe in the gods at all!

'Agnostics' are different from atheists. They claim that they do not know whether there is any kind of god or not. They tend to say that questions like whether God exists, and whether there is life after death, cannot be answered. We do not have any proof of such things, they say. Such things cannot be established by the scientific method. They like to leave such things – so they say – to the private opinions of each individual. They dislike the idea that there should be any teaching about such matters in schools. Each person has to make up his own mind (they say) and no one must force his opinion about such things upon others – although the opinion that no god is known to exist may (so they seem to think) be forcefully pressed on others.

Every outlook on life is a matter of some kind of 'faith'. The Christian and the atheist both have a circle of ideas which are worth comparing and contrasting. Atheists are taking a position of 'faith'. They trust that there is no God. They feel that the evidence is lacking, and that a certain kind of scientific proof is needed before we can say that there is God, so their position is one of trust.

What are the alternatives?

1. Is it that the world has sprung from nowhere? There is no god. There once was nothing-nothing-nothing and somehow our universe came into being out of nothing-nothing-nothing. There seems to be no one who believes this!

2. Is it that the world sprang from something impersonal? Is it that the stuff of the universe has somehow always existed, and at some stage out of sheer luck or chance or coincidence there was some kind of collision of particles of energy or some kind of impersonal 'big bang' and out of the primitive chop-suey mixture came the universe and our world and men and women themselves, with their sense of God, their conscience, their awareness of right and wrong, their sense of beauty, their longing for purpose and fulfilment and destiny? Are we to believe it all came by totally impersonal forces, combinations of powers and forces and currents of energy or whatever? Are we to believe the universe has always been there, but some kind of lucky undirected, ungoverned combination, like the spin of the wheel at the casino, took place and somehow produced humanity? Is that what we are to believe?

3. Or are we to believe the origin of our universe is in God or the gods? Can we believe that our universe has a personal origin? Is there some kind of God who is back behind everything?

If God is behind everything, what kind of God or gods are we to believe in? Are we to believe in impersonal gods? It is rather difficult to decide whether some eastern faiths are forms of religion or forms of atheism. This is because the god that is being believed in is not personal. Often the god, it seems, is 'it' rather than 'he' or 'she'.

Are we to believe in some kind of polytheism? Are there gods and goddesses with their varied characteristics? Is there an out-of-reach impersonal deity with dozens of gods under it? Are there Vishnu, Shiva, Krishna, Ganesh, and dozens – even thousands or millions of minor deities in addition?

Then what do we think about behaviour? Which of the various possibilities give us a sense of responsibility? Which take away responsibility? Which feel clean? And which feel dirty? Which elevate human life? And which degrade human life?

Then what do we think about knowledge? Can we really know God? Can we know anything? If I see millions of particulars is there anything that holds them together? If everything is one is there any way of making particular distinctions? Can I see any unity in the world? Is it all a mass of random fragments?

The Christian claim is that God made the world. He is there. He is real. It is possible to talk to him. It is possible to hear him. He is the living God. He speaks. He has acted in human history. He has sent Jesus. He has created his people, the living true church consisting of all people who know Jesus as alive.

Everyone has to explain the fact that the world exists and that within the world men and women exist and that there is something very special and unique about men and women. Language exists. Communication exists. Right and wrong exist. Even those who do not have any grounds for believing in right and wrong soon complain if you injure them or steal something from them.

The fact is: our world needs explaining. Where did it come from ultimately? We human beings also need explaining. Where do we come from? If we evolved, what or who steered the evolution?

Atheists have various arguments against the existence of God. One is the reality of evil. And the other is the idea that God is an unnecessary hypothesis. These two problems have been around for a long time. Thomas Aquinas was trying to deal with them six hundred years ago. There are other matters that need some kind of overview. We are aware of the reality of guilt, the value of pain, the solidarity between creation and man, the concern for our ultimate destiny, our anxiety about life after death. Atheism has been a non-theistic religion. It requires faith. It was one of the results of the Enlightenment when people started trusting entirely in human reason to philosophize themselves, in explaining every aspect of human life, including God. But the anti-god mentality of the late-western culture has not improved the quality of human understanding. It is time we listened to the biblical description of God, and began to find out for ourselves what the truth is. God reveals himself so that we shall 'feel after' him or 'grope after' him. God is not very far away. In Jesus, God is able to be found.

SIX

Can Human Language Cope with God?

In the twentieth century, religious language has been reckoned a difficult matter. This has come about because of the rise of 'logical positivism' which arose through the philosophy of Ludwig Wittgenstein and the Vienna Circle. The main idea behind 'logical positivism' was the notion that if a statement is not verifiable it is meaningless. Many religious claims – it is argued – are unverifiable and therefore they are meaningless.

A.J. Ayer developed Wittgenstein's ideas. In *Language, Truth and Logic* (1936) he argued that there are only two types of statement, analytic and synthetic. Analytic statements are 'tautologies', statements that are true by definition (like 'A triangle has three sides'). Others are 'synthetic statements', and these are only meaningful (Ayer argued) if they are verifiable or (as he said later) falsifiable.

It was pointed out that the verification principle is itself not verifiable! Ayer made certain changes in his theory and in the second edition of his work talked about 'falsifiability' rather than verification. Yet still his theory is open to objections. Some scientific statements might be quite meaningful but hard to verify or falsify. Also some historical statements might be hard to verify. Also some claims about value or about beauty might be quite meaningful but hard to verify or falsify. 'Mrs Kamau is a very beautiful lady' is a statement with a meaning, but there might be disagreements about it and it might be hard to prove in a way with which everyone would agree!

Karl Barth's theology is in some ways similar (although Ayer

and Barth would not have liked to be compared with each other).
Barth's God is 'wholly other' and is entirely outside the area of
what is verifiable.

A better approach to religious language is that of analogy.
The way in which the thirteenth century theologian, Thomas
Aquinas, put the matter is much more convincing – although I
hasten to add that I am not generally a Thomist. Aquinas said
that when we speak about God we speak of him in a human way,
using analogy. Humankind is, according to Christians, made in
the image of God. For this reason there is some correspondence
and comparison between God and the human race. So we may
use human language in talking about God.

We also use analogy. When we use an ordinary word to refer
to God (e.g. father) we are not using the word in exactly the same
way ('univocal') as when we are talking of other things, nor in
a totally different way ('equivocal'). When we call God father,
there is an analogy, a similarity between a human father and the
fatherhood of God. By using many analogies we talk about God.
When we use language about God we are not using a 'wholly
other' meaning. Yet we are not using a totally this-world meaning. We are using analogy. We use names and descriptions. It is
possible to put into words something of what we know of God.
For example, the Bible does put things into human language. We
use picture language. We call God king. We say he loves, he
forgives. We have some idea of what these words mean. They
are used in everyday speech and we apply them to God. God
puts into the Scriptures statements about himself that are true.

The Christian (for example) says he knows God, not only in
a hidden, eerie, wholly mysterious manner, but confidently and
openly. 'I know him whom I have believed,' said Paul (2 Tim.
1:12). It is not simply a knowledge of doctrine or philosophy that
he refers to. Paul writes 2 Timothy in prison but he is not at all
distressed or ashamed to be there. He knows God! He gives
thanks to him as to a personal friend (2 Tim. 1:3). He is conscious
of love and power and self-discipline coming as a gift from the
heavenly Father (2 Tim. 1:7). He is willing to suffer for the God
who has saved him. He has entrusted his eternal salvation to the
God he knows as a father, and boldly and confidently says, 'I am
convinced that he is able to guard what I have entrusted to him

for that day'. But the language he is using is the language of analogy.

Aquinas' approach to religious language seems to be correct although it perhaps needs to be updated and restated to meet modern problems and modern questions. The position seems to be as follows:

1. Ayer was mistaken in limiting meaningful statements to only two categories. There are other kinds of statement that are not tautologies, not empirically verifiable, and yet are quite meaningful. Statements concerning beauty, justice, ethics, certain aspects of astronomical science, history, and other matters cannot pass the strictness of Ayer's requirements yet they seem to be quite meaningful.

2. Ayer does not seem to consider the possibility that verification might lie in the future. The Christian maintains that God's verification will be future. It will be at the Day of Judgment. Then – argues the Christian – men and women will get all the verification they need.

There is a parable told by B.G. Mitchell, which I like. I can retell it and rewrite as follows[1]:

> A certain country is invaded by its enemies. It is defeated and occupied by its enemies. Yet there is a 'resistance movement' and citizens of the country work secretly to overthrow the enemies who have invaded them.
>
> One night a member of the resistance movement meets a stranger who deeply impresses him. They spend that night together in conversation. The Stranger tells the resistance worker that he himself is on the side of the resistance. Indeed He is in command of it. He urges the resistance worker to have total faith in Him no matter what happens. The Stranger becomes a friend. The resistance worker is utterly convinced at his meeting with the Stranger, that his new Friend is utterly sincere, and totally trustworthy. He promises to trust in his new Friend. They do not often meet in quite such freedom again. Sometimes the Friend is seen helping members of the resistance movement. The resistance worker is grateful and tells his colleagues, 'He is on our side'.

Sometimes the Friend is seen in the uniform of the police handing over patriots to the occupying power. On these occasions members of the resistance complain and criticize. But the resistance worker still says 'He is on our side'. He still believes that in spite of appearances, the Friend did not deceive him. Sometimes he asks the Friend for help and he receives it. He is then thankful. Sometimes he asks for help and he does not receive it. Then he says 'The Friend knows best'. Sometimes his colleagues complain in exasperation, 'Well, if *that's* what you mean by his being on our side, the sooner he goes over to the other side the better!'

Yet the resistance worker does not allow anything to count against the proposition, 'The Friend is on our side'. This is because he has committed himself to trust the Stranger who became the Friend.

One point of this parable – and there are others – is the vindication lies in the future. While a war is going on the friend of the member of the resistance has to be trusted. Yet he knows that one day the war will be over and all his mysterious behaviour will be explained. The Christian believes something like this with regard to God. For him or her, verification is future, and the story of the human race is not yet finished. Meanwhile the Christian knows his Friend so well that he is willing to trust Him, no matter what!

When we talk about knowing God, the question of verifiability comes into it in more than one way. Our total experience of God is involved.

In this connection the gospel of Luke is interesting. In the gospel of Luke there are two approaches to verification and meaningfulness. On the one hand Luke points to eyewitness testimony concerning the resurrection. There is an appeal to historical facts that (if they are accepted) point to something far above the natural, the non-miraculous, the scientifically verifiable. The resurrection of Jesus is a kind of verification. Luke wants partly to base faith on evidences. Jesus' death and resurrection are capable of historical investigation.

On the other hand Luke also wants his readers to come to faith in Jesus without being able to follow the historical reasoning that might be needed for the purposes of verification. Faith in the eye-witness testimony of the apostles, faith in the Word of God, also brings with it a kind of proof or verification. The apostles on the Day of Pentecost received the Holy Spirit when they responded in faith to the message concerning Jesus. Christians today claim that they know God in a way that verifies to them that God is real. Yet religious experience is not the only verification. Historical investigation is possible as well.

Aquinas has shown that we use analogy in speaking about God. This does not answer every question but it is a starting point.

Historical investigation is also a kind of study in verifiability although historical verifiability does not fit into Ayer's two categories of language.

Personal experience of God, answered prayer, and other forms of religious experience must also be allowed to add their word of testimony. In such a way it is possible to speak about God. The Christian knows God, and he is able to put into words what he knows.

Endnote

1. My re-written version is based on the quotation in Mascall, E.L. *Words and Images: A Study in Theological Discourse* (Longmans, 1957) pp. 20–21.

PART TWO: KNOWING GOD

SEVEN

Knowing God: Principles

The thought that it might be possible to know God is staggering. Is it really possible? Can God be known? If so, to what extent? How much is it possible to know him? Can he be known personally? Can one put one's knowledge of him into words? There are a number of principles we should keep in mind:

1.   There is a universal knowledge of God. We have already seen that in one sense everyone is aware deep within that God is there. This revelation is apart from the Bible, apart from apostles, prophets and teachers. This is distinct from his plan of salvation. It is sometimes called general revelation (because it is everywhere) or natural revelation (because it comes through nature).

In Roman Catholic teaching the idea of God revealing himself universally in nature leads to what is called 'natural theology'. This is the idea that you can build teaching about God out of what is in nature, without the use of God's revelation in Jesus. But this is unbiblical. General revelation is a biblical idea. 'Natural theology' is not a biblical idea at all. General revelation is a fact but you cannot build on it to make a theology.

This general revelation comes (i) through all created things. 'The heavens declare the glory of God; the skies proclaim the work of his hands' (Ps. 19:1, see 19:1–4). It comes (ii) through God's watchful care of the world. Acts 14:16–17 speaks of the way in which God has created the world and also watches over it. 'He has not left himself without witness,' says Paul, 'by giving you rain from heaven and crops in their season'. God's care for the world gives man a sense that God is there. The Lord is good to all (Ps. 145:9; Matt. 5:45), and that gives everyone a sense of God.

This general revelation comes (iii) through what we call conscience. Men and women not only know that God is there; they also 'know God's righteous decree' that those who live wickedly deserve exclusion from God's blessing (see Rom. 1:32). When Amos addresses the nations in Amos 1:2–2:16 he mentions the law of God only when he is speaking to Judah (Amos 2:4–5) and to Israel (Amos 2:6–16). Israel and Judah sinned against the law of God (Amos 2:4) or against what God did for them at the time of the Exodus (Amos 2:10) or against the prophets (Amos 2:11). But what about the other nations? What about Damascus (Amos 1:3–5), Gaza (Amos 1:6–8), Tyre (Amos 1:9–10), Edom (Amos 1:11–12) and Ammon (Amos 1:13–14)? Amos does not quote the law of Moses to them. They have not sinned against God's law. They have sinned against conscience. Because they are human beings, they know that their sins were wicked. God is known through conscience even when he is not known through written law.

This 'general revelation' is to be found everywhere (Ps. 19:1–4). It is clear (Rom. 1:20–21). It explains the sense of God that all people have. It is the reason why even those who have not heard the gospel are still responsible before God. Even in their rebellion men and women have not totally escaped God. General revelation explains also the elements of truth in pagan religions, and in pagan morality (1 Cor. 5:1–2).

This general revelation becomes a special blessing after a person has become a Christian. For the Christian then views God's creation in the light of further revelation. In the Old Testament we have nature psalms (Pss. 8, 19, 65, 104) which praise God because of his glories in creation. The book of Job does something similar (see Job 38–41 especially). Isaiah 40:12–26 does the same.

2. A second principle is a contrast to the first. There is a universal ignorance of God. Although everyone knows God in one way, not everyone knows God in a personal way. The person who does not have faith in Jesus does not know God (1 Cor. 1:21). Man does not know God by wisdom. This kind of personal knowledge comes only through Jesus (John 17:3). Pagan religions are idolatrous. In conversion men and women turn from idols to serve the living God (1 Thess. 1:9–10). God is

known only through Jesus. He is the only way. God may only be approached through him (John 14:6).

The voice of God in nature is sufficient to condemn us but not sufficient to save us (Rom. 1:18ff). Jesus is still the only way to God (Matt. 11:27; John 14:6; 17:3; Acts 4:12). This general revelation does not rival revelation in Christ because it shows us how much we need Jesus. This voice of God in creation brings down the anger of God because everyone suppresses it. It is not redeeming. Paganism is darkness (Isa. 9:2; 41:29; Eph. 4:17; Acts 19:26; 1 Cor. 8:4).

The voice of God in nature is non-verbal. It has no words in it. This revelation is always suppressed by the natural man. It is part of his sin that he suppresses what he knows. It is the grounds of his condemnation, without his having heard God's written word. It is the reason why he needs forgiveness in and through the gospel message of Jesus Christ.

One cannot build on God's voice in creation. There is no such thing as natural theology. Roman Catholicism built much of its theology upon reason and natural theology. This is a mistake.

In Acts 14:15–17 Paul pointed to God's oneness (14:15), God's power (14:15), God's patience (14:16), God's kindness (14:17). God is there! Upon the sure and certain basis that God is there Paul asked his listeners to turn to the living God. It was his 'good news' that God could be known. You get to know God by dealing with him directly. By speaking to him. By listening to him. Idolatry is a great sin. Every person is judged according to whether or not he was an idolater.

A Christian not only believes in God. He believes God. He believes God's word. The way to know God is to submit to what God says about Jesus. It is to receive his offer of Jesus as Saviour. Without Jesus the voice of God in nature does not lead to the deeper knowledge of God. In and through Jesus God can be known personally.

3. Another principle is: God is known as he reveals himself. If God did not reveal himself no one would know him personally. He reveals himself through nature and creation, but more intimately in Jesus. This is checked and confirmed through the Scriptures. Men and women try to get through to God through wisdom and intelligence and 'experiences' but the only way to

God is through Jesus, as God works by the Spirit and as we respond to him.

Jesus said, 'All things have been handed over to me by my Father' (Matt. 11:27). Jesus has authority over every aspect of creation and every aspect of God's salvation. Jesus went on, '. . . and no one knows the Son except the Father'. The greatness of Jesus as a Saviour is so great that only God can fathom its depths. Then Jesus says, '. . . and no one knows the Father except the Son'. Just as the Son of God is so great that only the Father can appreciate him, so the Father is so great that only the Son of God, Jesus, can appreciate him. But Jesus goes further: '. . . and no one knows the Father except the Son, and he to whom the Son is willing to reveal him' God is staggeringly, overwhelmingly beyond our knowledge. Yet Jesus knows the Father, and Jesus is willing to share with us what he knows. Knowing God is utterly and totally dependent on God's revealing himself to us through Jesus.

4. It is possible to speak about God. When thinking about God it is possible to make use of human language. It might be thought that God is so devastatingly mysterious that human language is incapable of saying anything about him. If God is so great one might ask how is it possible to speak of him? Perhaps it is impossible, we might think, to put our thinking about God into human words.

Yet the Bible has plenty to say about God and is not hesitant about putting plenty of pronouncements about what God is like. The biblical writers were quite confident that they could put ideas about God into human language. We are using analogy. We use names and descriptions. It is possible to put into words something of what we know of God. The Bible does put things into human language. We use picture language. We call God king. We say he loves, he forgives. We have some idea of what these words mean. They are used in everyday speech and we apply them to God. God puts into the Scriptures statements about himself that are true.

So what we are seeing is the wonderful possibility of knowing about God, not only in a hidden, eerie, wholly mysterious manner, but confidently and openly. 'I know him whom I have believed,' said Paul (2 Tim. 1:12). It is not simply a knowledge of doctrine or philosophy that he refers to. He writes 2 Timothy in prison but he is not at all distressed or ashamed to be there. He knows God! He gives thanks to him as a personal friend (2 Tim. 1:3). He is conscious of love and power and self-discipline coming as a gift from the heavenly Father (2 Tim. 1:7). He is willing to suffer for the God who has saved him. He has entrusted his eternal salvation to the God he knows as a father, and boldly and confidently says 'I am convinced that he is able to guard what I have entrusted to him for that day'.

5. Knowledge of God is partial and progressive. We get to know God more and more. However we never come to know him exhaustively. There are secret things about God that no one knows or appreciates. In Deuteronomy 29, the people are being summoned to be utterly loyal to God. Moses reviews Israel's history reminding them of the Lord's great works in days gone by (29:1–9). Then he urges them to be committed to obey God's covenant (29:10–15). He warns them that curses will come on covenant-breakers (29:16–28). Then Moses says: 'The secret things belong to the LORD our God, but the things that are revealed belong to us and to our children forever, so that we might keep all the words of this law' (Deut. 29:29). There are things about God and his will that are hidden. We do not know everything. We are dependent on revelation. Moses says the commands of God are revealed, but there are things about God which are not revealed. They belong to God and not to us.

Isaiah 55:8–9 says 'For my thoughts are not your thoughts, neither are your ways my ways. As the heavens are higher than the earth, so are my ways higher than your ways and my thoughts higher than your thoughts'. God is above us. His ways are past finding out. We do get to know God but we do not get to know him exhaustively.

Other passages of Scripture make the same point: 1 Corinthians 2:10–12, Psalm 139:6, 17, 145:3; 147:5; Romans 11:33, Job 26:14; 11:7–9; 37:5. We do not fully understand God or any one thing about him. Yet knowledge of God may be real and it is to be always increasing (Col. 1:10). We are to seek God; and we shall find him. But to say this is to say that our knowledge of God is to progress. We are to get to know his ways. We shall know him even more in the final glory.

6. Also, our knowledge of God has to be a personal practical living experience. Knowledge of God is encountering him, meeting him. It is a highly practical and life-changing experience. It leads to understanding other matters. The fear of the LORD is the beginning of wisdom (Prov. 9:10). It leads to an understanding of ourselves, and of the world. It results in our acting boldly for God. 'The people who know their God shall stand firm and take action' (Dan. 11:32).

EIGHT

The Presence of God

We now take a step forward and consider the practicalities of knowing God. We can come at the matter from five angles. We must consider (i) beginning with bare faith, (ii) the habit of honesty, (iii) enjoying God's presence, (iv) seeking God's will, and (v) knowing God's ways.

There is a difference between knowing God and knowing *about* God. It is good to know *about* God but we are talking about something greater and higher. The generation of Jewish leaders who crucified Jesus knew a lot about God but they did not know God.

Sometimes people speak of 'knowing God', when really what they are talking or writing about is knowing *about* God. I am trying to speak and write about both knowing about God and knowing God. Knowing God includes knowing about him but it is more. It is knowing him in a practical and experiential way. How does it come about in our experience?

1. We have to begin with bare faith. You already know that God is there, but now you have to believe what he says. You begin with what I would like to call sheer faith or naked faith or bare faith. You believe the facts of the gospel. You believe that Jesus is the Son of God. You believe that Jesus died for you upon the cross. You acknowledge that you are a sinner. You don't try to justify yourself. You cast yourself entirely upon the mercy of God. Believe that you are accepted. You do not deserve anything. God reveals himself to you by pure grace (see Acts 16:31; Rom. 4:4; 11: 6). The Philippian jailer did not need a course or any kind of preparation. He had to believe by bare faith.

See how the father received his son in Luke 15:17–24. He

refused to let his son say, 'Make me one of your hired servants'. Romans 4:5: 'To him that does nothing but believes . . .'. You start by relating to God by sheer faith. Do not worry about your unworthiness. Accept God's grace. Believe you are accepted no matter what you feel. Put trust before feelings.

There is no way to know God except through Jesus (John. 14:6). You are not commanded to seek God at this point. There is no seeking involved in this. Believe! Respond to the command of Paul in Acts 16:31. No preparation or time is needed. Believe – and believe now!

2.   A second matter is the habit of honesty. The fact is that many of us who say we want to know God are actually scared of being honest in God's presence. Honesty is a scary thing! But fellowship with God comes by walking in the light. After you have been saved by trusting Jesus and his cross, you begin to seek the Lord. You will need to 'walk in the light', as John puts it in 1 John 1.

You realize the purity of God. 'God is light and in him there is no darkness at all'. We are seeking to know God. We must remember what God is like. When you are seeking to befriend someone you remember what they are like, what they approve of, what they disapprove of. God is light. He is holiness, purity. He hates sin.

You avoid pretence. 'If we say we are having fellowship with him but we are walking in darkness, we lie'. We must not claim to be in fellowship with God if at this very moment we are not enjoying fellowship with God. We must not over-claim. We must not pretend we are knowing God if at the moment our relationship to him has been spoiled.

You walk in the light of God's holiness and God's will. 'If we walk in the light . . .'. To walk in the light means to act upon anything God shows us.

If you live this way you will be enjoying fellowship. Something will happen. We shall have fellowship. With the Father and the Son. With each other. God will be faithful. He will forgive sin. He will cleanse away the stain. He will give us a clear conscience and a happy relationship with himself.

This is the starting point in knowing God. We must have a happy conscience, a consciousness of fellowship with God.

It is at this point that you might want to draw back! You said you wanted to know God, but now the question is pressed upon you. Do you really want to know God? Knowing God is a matter of walking in the light! God is a good friend but sometimes his friendship is painful and costly. He is a friend who will tell you the truth about yourself and you might not always want to be told what he will tell you.

3. Walking in the light persistently, is sometimes called 'the practice of the presence of God'. It is possible to enjoy God's presence all day long. It is possible to be enjoying him when you are at work or in the kitchen or in the office, or when you are writing a letter or preparing a lesson for school.

With ordinary friends – if they are good friends – you are able to enjoy being with someone without having to be talking all the time. It is also possible to relate to God in the same way. There is such a thing as relating to God as to a friend. God wants to be a friend to us.

It involves knowing that you are covered with the righteousness of Jesus. You will never be able to enjoy God's friendship unless you know that he has dealt with all of your sins. You must know that you are secure in his grace, that your relationship with him is maintained by God himself. You are not keeping yourself in the Christian life. Jesus is keeping you.

Enjoying the presence of God is a matter of *persistently* walking in the light. Enjoying God's presence and walking in the light are not different things, but I want to make the point that it is possible to walk in the light *constantly* and enjoy God's presence *constantly*. You must know that he has no quarrel with you. Any particular thing he has spoken to you about, you have to put right.

You begin each day by coming into the presence of God. It does not take a long time. It is a matter of believing that he accepts you, knowing that the blood of Jesus covers your sins, knowing that the righteousness of Jesus gives you right of access to God. You act upon anything he is asking of you. You confess anything he is pointing out to you. Know that God sympathizes with you. He is touched by your weaknesses.

Have the Lord always before you. David said in Psalm 16:8, 'I have set the LORD always before me. Because he is at my right hand I shall not be shaken'. Know that God is there with you. Feel him. Enjoy his love. We are meant to enjoy the presence of God. This is not the same as feeling happy. Feelings of ease and happiness come and go. They let us down in times of tiredness, sickness, old age, death. Happy feelings may go up and down but there should generally be the deep peace of knowing that God is with us. Refuse to be anxious about anything. Obey the challenge of Philippians 4:6,7. Keep a clear conscience by the blood of Jesus Christ (Heb. 9:14).

Then, fourthly, the true Christian, the saved person, must seek God. You might think that if you are saved you do not need to seek God because you have found him. But actually you still need to seek to know God more. God likes it when we seek him.

The commands in the Bible to seek God are addressed to Christians or to Israel. We have commands to seek God and his will (see Matt. 6:33; 7:7,8; Luke 12:31; Acts 15:17; 17:27; Rom. 2:7; Heb. 11:6). Matthew 13:45 is a parable about seeking the blessings of the kingdom.

What is involved in seeking God? Give God time. Knowing God is a two-way matter. You must listen as well as speak. It takes time to seek God. Some time each day (an hour?). Some time each week (several hours one day a week?). Some time each month (one Saturday a month?). Some time each year (the first week of the year?). Work out how you do it for yourself – but you will have to find a way of giving God time.

Enjoying God involves asking God questions. You ask him questions about what has happened. It is like the story of Rebekah in Genesis 25:22. She is expecting a baby, but finds strange movements within her body. She goes to God and asks, 'Why is this happening to me?' It led to God speaking to her (Gen. 25:23). To seek God involves asking questions about his will (as, for example in Judg. 1:1–2). Maybe it will be a question with a yes/no answer (as in 2 Sam. 2:1a). Maybe it will lead into further questioning (as in 2 Sam. 2:1b).

Seeking God involves sharing your heart with God. You share your painful experiences (like Hannah in 1 Sam. 1). You talk about your needs (Phil. 4:9). You ask him about the desires of your heart concerning his kingdom.

Seeking God involves praying with every kind of prayer. You

worship him; you thank him; you bring your petitions to him; you intercede for others.

Another aspect of getting to know God – the fifth of my list – is learning God's ways. We are told that after God saved Israel by the blood of the lamb he wanted to bring them into all of his promises. They had to go on believing God amidst many crises. However the people of Israel again and again lapsed into unbelief. Finally God got angry with them, because Israel 'did not know his ways' (Heb. 3:10).

God has ways. He has habits in the way in which he deals with us. He has a habit of putting us into crises, but we must discover that the crises we experience are not as bad as they seem. This is what happened to the Israelites in the wilderness. As we learn about God we are discovering that God has a habit of testing us. We have to learn not to panic.

We also discover that God has a habit of sending help in the time of need but not before. We are given grace to help in the time of need (Heb. 4:16), not before and not too late. We find that God has a habit of answering prayer but he tends to delay and get us ready for the answer before he sends it. We have to be ready for answered prayer.[1] It is possible to pray but not get ready for the answer. In Acts 12:12–16 we find the church diligently at prayer but amazed at getting the answer to their prayers! The church was young and inexperienced and God forgave them. But when a mature believer did the same thing he was severely rebuked (Luke 1:18–20).

God has a habit of working all things together for Good. Romans 8:28 means that when everything is going wrong, everything is going right! God works everything together for good. Does this include bad things? Yes! Romans 8 refers to 'present sufferings' (v.18), and to ignorance and 'weaknesses' (v.26). Does it even include our sins? Yes! Jonah's sin was overruled to get some sailors saved (Jonah 1). Peter's sin at Antioch led to the writing of Galatians (see Gal. 2:11–14). Jesus' death was wicked in itself but was used by God (Acts 2:23). The same principle is in Genesis 50:20. The biggest hindrance to knowing God is a bad conscience about the past. Believe in Romans 8:28! Leave the past with God. Know him now and forget the past, no matter how bad it has been. Press on to achieve something for him. Forget what is behind. Aim at the will of God that lies ahead. Seek the prize for achieving something for God (Phil. 3:13–16).

Endnote

1. See R.T. Kendall's sermon, 'Answered Prayer' in *Ready for God* (Scripture Union, 1995), pp. 11–18.

NINE

Living on God

At this point in my little book I am feeling overwhelmed! The rest of what I want to say involves this entire matter of living on God. The reason why we want to know about God is because we want to know God himself! You get to know the LORD and as you do so you are remembering and learning more and more what he is really like.

Every aspect of who and what God is affects how we get to know him. Our descriptions of what God is like are simply ways of putting into words what we have learned about him in experience.

Because God is spirit (John 4:20–24), you do not get too bothered about ritual and places of worship and ceremony. Because God is one (Deut. 6:4), you loathe the thought of giving any sort of worship to anything or anyone less than God. God alone rules your heart. Because of God's self-sufficiency (Acts 17:25), you find your own personal adequacy in God. Because of God's personal-ness, or personality, you talk to him and relate to him as friend-with-friend.

There is a vast difference between getting excited about theology and living on God! It is easy to confuse the two. It is possible to have great and wonderful intellectual ideas about the sovereignty of God and then fall to pieces when some tiny little problem appears. It is possible to believe that God's kingdom rules over everything (Ps. 103:19) and that if we ask anything according to his will he hears us (1 John 5:14) and then panic in alarm and distress when we lose our keys! It is possible to pray that a friend will be released from prison and then refuse to believe that he is outside knocking at the door (Acts 12:5, 12–16).

We are to learn to live on God! His unchangeability means that we shall not be consumed (Mal. 3:6). His power (Jer. 32:17) means that nothing is impossible for him. His being the living God (Heb. 9:14) means that we come alive with the liveliness of God himself. God's vastness (Jer. 23:24) means that we cannot hide from him. His eternity (Ps. 90:2) calls us to seek that he will establish the work of our hands for us (Ps. 90:17). God's knowledge (Ps. 139:1–6) produces humility and a desire that he will reveal to us the truth about ourselves (Ps. 139:23).

Every aspect of God's character is practical. It is entirely worthless to follow doctrinal interests if we are not living on God himself. Our thinking is not academic theorizing. It is meditating on the wonderful ways of God. It is to lead to rejoicing, praising, worshipping. It is to produce in us confidence, poise, stability, trustworthiness, sincerity, affection, compassion, warmth. It is to release us from timidity, anxiety, resentment. God's wisdom (Dan. 2:20) leads to our wisdom. God's truthfulness (Titus 1:2) leads to our truthfulness. God's faithfulness (1 Cor. 1:9) leads to our faithfulness. God's love (Rom. 5:8) leads to our love.

What richness there is in God. As we move on with God, we find out by our experience of him, what he is like. If we are walking in the Spirit, giving God time, meditating day and night on the ways of God we become 'like a tree planted by streams of water, which yields its fruit in season, and whose leaf does not wither'. We ponder the lessons of God's mercy, God's grace, God's patience, his long-suffering, compassion, goodness, holiness, righteousness, and if we are truly walking with God, to know what he is like will affect us.

But it is not only the nice aspects of God's character that affect us. We know of God's anger (Rom. 1:18) against the sins of the world, and yet we know God has been propitiated and his anger towards us has turned aside by the cross of Jesus. Yet we have discovered the way God feels about sin. We know that although he will not abandon us we can vex him, and he can discipline us in his displeasure. It produces in us the 'fear of the Lord', an intense desire not to displease him. We know of God's jealousy, his refusal to tolerate a rival to him in our lives.

Then there is something about God which is almost impossible to put into words. The Bible speaks of God's exaltedness, God's greatness, God's excellency, God's beauty, God's glory, God's blessedness. God is extraordinary. God is happy with himself. God is shiningly beautiful.

It should not surprise us that the Bible is a book full of music. When you are beginning to get to know God it somehow comes out in song and in music! The intellectual side of human nature is not adequate to express how we feel about God, and somehow we have to put it into melody and tunefulness. There comes a kind of swing in our lives, a kind of rhythm. We are rejoicing in God! As soon as Israel were redeemed by the blood of the lamb, melody came into their lives! Exodus 12–14 (the Passover) was followed by Exodus 15 and they started singing:

> I will sing to the LORD,
> for he is highly exalted.
> The horse and its rider
> He has hurled into the sea!

> The Lord is my strength and my song;
> He has become my salvation.
> He is my God and I will praise him,
> my father's God and I will exalt him.

Then they started dancing. It was not organized or programmed. It was the spontaneous joyousness of people who had experienced the mighty deliverances of God. Miriam was so overjoyed, she went and found a tambourine and started dancing. All the women followed her. Miriam was leading the singing:

> Sing to the LORD,
> for he is highly exalted.
> The horse and its rider
> He has hurled into the sea!

This is what it means to know God! It leads to vibrant energy for God, a mood of confidence and joy. It leads to audacity and daring. It leads to contentment and peace.[1]

Endnote

1. See the excellent chapter, 'The People Who Know Their God' in Packer, J. I. *Knowing God* (Hodder, 1975), pp. 21–30.

PART THREE:
GOD THE THREE-IN-ONE

TEN

Experiencing God's Threeness

All doctrine must be thought about experientially and practically. In all of our thoughts and all of our studies we must remember that we are thinking of how we experience God. Teaching or doctrine must not be just an intellectual matter.

We now come to think of how we experience our God as three-in-one.[1] Let us begin with a basic statement. The Bible presents us with a picture of God who is three and one at the same time. This is often called the Trinity. Trinity is not a Bible word in itself, but it is a word that we use to summarize a number of things that are taught about God in the Bible. Muslims and Jehovah's Witnesses and other cults stumble over this doctrine of the Trinity. It is the greatest mystery in the Christian faith. It is quite impossible to understand it by pure intellectual ability. Indeed, it is worth remembering that no one would ever have had a reason for inventing the doctrine of the Trinity. The only reason we believe it is because God has revealed that this is what he is.

There are basically seven things that are involved in what we call the doctrine of the Trinity:

1. We scarcely need to argue that according to the Bible there is only one God. It is something that is found all over the Bible although there are some explicit statements about the one-ness of God (Deut. 4:35; 6:4–5; 1 Ki. 8:60; 2 Ki. 19:15; Mark 12:29; John 17:3; Rom. 3:30; 1 Cor. 8:4; 1 Tim. 2:5; Jam. 2:19).

2. God is presented as Father in relation to Jesus. 'There is to us one God, the Father', said Paul (1 Cor. 8:6). There is 'one God and Father' (Eph. 4:6). God is one; he may be viewed as distinct from the Son. In relation to the Son he is 'God and Father' (Eph.

1:3). The Son comes in the glory of 'his Father' (Mark 8:38). Jesus calls God 'my Father' (Luke 2:49; 12:32; 22:42; 23:34; 23:46; 24:49). He never uses the term 'our father' where the word 'our' includes himself. Jesus has a unique sonship; God is his father in a unique way.

3.   Jesus is described as God and is called the Son in relation to God. There are verses in the Bible which actually call Jesus 'God'. John 1:1 says '. . . and the Word was God'. John 1:18 says of Jesus that he is 'the one and only God'. In John 20:28 Thomas worships Jesus as 'my Lord and my God'. Romans 9:5 says that from the Jewish people 'is the Christ . . . God over all'. Hebrews 1:8 addresses Jesus when it says, 'Your throne, O God is for ever and ever'. Titus 2:13 speaks of 'our great God and Saviour'. 2 Peter 1:1 talks of 'the righteousness of our God and Saviour Jesus Christ'. 1 John 5:20 says 'He is the true God'. Philippians 2:5–8 and Colossians 1:15–20 have similar teaching.

Many of these verses are disputed. However, although this is not the place to go into the discussions in detail, in every case the translation for which there is the best evidence is one which implies that Jesus is God. There are other passages where the translation is more doubtful, and some which are textually unreliable.[2]

But there is other evidence besides that of direct statements of Christ's deity. Jesus acted in such a way that implied he was God. He 'was calling God his own Father, making himself equal with God' (John 5:18). The disciples came to see the meaning of his names and titles, such as Lord and Son of God. They came slowly to realize that they imply that he is one with God and equally to be worshipped. God has a Son. The Son of God was there before his birth. God sent one who already was his divine Son.

The works of Jesus are divine works. Jesus is equal to the Father in works of creation, judgment and salvation. Also the disciples worshipped Jesus. They would say things like 'To him be the glory both now and for ever!' (2 Pet. 3:18). Or 'to him that loves us . . . to him be glory and dominion for ever and ever' (Rev. 1:5b, 6; see also 2 Tim. 4:18; Heb. 13:20–21; Rev. 5:13). We find that the early Christians prayed to Jesus (Acts 7:59, 60) and said, 'Let all God's angels worship him' (Heb. 1:6).

4. The Spirit is God. To lie to the Spirit is to lie to God (Acts 5:3,4). To have the Spirit within our personalities is to be the temple of God (1 Cor. 6:19–20). The Spirit has divine characteristics. He is eternal (Heb. 9:14). He knows everything (1 Cor. 2:10–11). He is all-present (Ps. 139:7). He is all-powerful (Luke 1:35,39). The Spirit participates in the divine works of creation, regeneration, inspiration, resurrection. To blaspheme his testimony is to blaspheme unforgivably (Mark 3:28–29). The Spirit is personal. He does personal things. He can be grieved. He can be angered. He leads and guides and speaks. In the book of Acts he forbids, he approves, he bears witness and is tested by sin, and is resisted. The entire presentation of the Spirit is that he is a divine personal being.

5. The Father is not the Son. God sent the Son. The Son prays to the Father. The Son of God is in some way distinct from the Father.

6. The Father is not the Spirit. Think of the story of Jesus' baptism. The Father sends the Spirit upon the Son.

7. The Son is not the Spirit. The Spirit glorifies the Son. He comes down upon the Son, but he is not himself the person of the Son of God.

It is this combination of seven truths about God that, when all put together, we call the doctrine of the Trinity.

Next, let us think about three heresies, three beliefs that are contradictions of the biblical teaching. The following are false ways of thinking about the Trinity:

1. It is not that there are three Gods. This would be the heresy of tritheism.

2. It is not that there is one God who takes different forms at different times. This is the heresy which scholars called modalism. Modalism denies that there are eternally three persons. It says that Father, Son and Spirit are three manifestations of one God. The idea is that God just appears in three forms. It is thought that God is one but appears in different ways and takes different modes of being, just as water can be ice at one moment, liquid water in the next moment, and steam a little later. But the three forms of water do not illustrate the Trinity; it illustrates the heresy of modalism! Actually finding illustrations of the Trinity is almost impossible. Modalism is false teaching. The Father, the

Son and the Spirit are distinct. Think of Jesus' baptism, and the way in which the Spirit came down upon the Son and the Father spoke from heaven.

3. It is not that Jesus or the Spirit are divine in an inferior way. This is the heresy of subordinationism. Subordinationism says that Father, Son and Spirit form a hierarchy, with the Father as the true God and Jesus and the Spirit as divine in some lesser sense. The idea is that Jesus and the Spirit are inferior kinds of deity. But again, this is false teaching. Jesus is not a junior God. Jesus is as much God as the Father is God. There is no subordinate deity. It is true that there is an order in their working but no person of the Trinity is less God than the Father.

We must think of three persons that are divine – but one God. Deity, God-ness, is in Jesus. Deity, God-ness is in the Holy Spirit. We worship the Son, we worship the Spirit, we worship the Father.

If you find this difficult, so do I. It is indeed a mysterious matter. But I can give you a hint about how to live with it! The best way to live with the doctrine of the Trinity is experientially. When we experience God we experience him as three-in-one. The doctrine is a great mystery. No philosopher could have invented this. The best way to understand it is in experience. Know God as your Father. Know Jesus and worship Jesus as God in the flesh, the one that died for you upon the cross, your Lord and your God. He is ever-living and makes intercession for you at the right hand of the Father. The Spirit is God within you. The Trinity is best understood experientially. Experience the Father. Experience Jesus as your Saviour. Experience the Spirit as your friend and as the one who empowers you. The many trinitarian passages of the Bible help us to approach the Trinity in this living and practical way.

We get to understand the Trinity as much as we ever will do by knowing that God loves us and has proved it by sending his Son. We see Jesus praying to the Father. We know that the Father cares for us as a father. He is indeed father-like. We know that Jesus is a brother to us. He is divine yet he is a fellow human being, and intercedes for us with the Father. We experience the power of the Spirit, and discover that the Spirit glorifies Jesus.

Let us consider a few trinitarian verses of the New Testament.

One of the greatest of them is Matthew 28:19 where in Jesus' last commission to his disciples he told them to go and make disciples, 'baptizing them into the name of the Father, the Son and the Holy Spirit'.[3] The new disciple expresses his faith in the fact that he is coming into fellowship with God. He expresses his faith by being water-baptized. When he comes to faith, expressed in water-baptism, he is coming 'into' God. From the time when he comes to faith and onwards, he expects to be experiencing fellowship with God. There is one God with one name. It does not say 'into the names' (plural), but into the 'name' (singular). In God there is Father, Son and Holy Spirit. In having fellowship with God the Christian is conscious of each member of the Trinity. We get to know God as our Father and Jesus as our Saviour. We know that the Father sent Jesus. We know that in some way God is in Jesus. The best way to understand the Trinity is to know God as our Father, and know Jesus as our divine Saviour. We worship Jesus as God. We know that Jesus died for us. We call him our Lord and our God. We know he ever lives to intercede for us. We know that the Father sends the Spirit as we call upon Jesus. We experience Jesus' pouring out the Spirit upon us, and we cry 'Father' to him as a result. As we get to know God we get to know him as Father, Son and Holy Spirit.

Or consider the statements of Paul in the letter to the Romans. We have peace with God through Jesus. God pours out his love in our hearts through the Spirit. What the Holy Spirit does, says Paul, is point us to the love of God in Jesus. God demonstrates his love in sending his Son. The Spirit floods out a sense of this love in our hearts (see Rom. 5:5,8).

Consider Romans 8:1–4,9,13–17. There is no condemnation for us because we are in Christ, the Son of God. God was the one who sent his Son to do for us what the law could not do. But then when we are in Christ we walk according to the Spirit. The Spirit is the Spirit of God. He is also the Spirit of Christ. He is the Spirit of God who raised Jesus from the dead. All of these statements are riddled through and through with allusion to the three persons, the Father, the Son and the Spirit. All of them are treated as God. We are led by the Spirit of God. This is part of our being the sons and daughters of God. It proves we are heirs with Christ.

Think of Romans 14:14–18, 'I know in the Lord Jesus that nothing is unclean in itself . . . The kingdom of God is . . . joy in the Spirit. He who serves Christ . . . is acceptable'. Paul easily mentions the Father, the Son and the Spirit in the same breath. In Romans 15:16 he speaks of being a 'minister of Jesus' and of 'the gospel of God' and of being 'sanctified by the Spirit'. This trinitarian language is typical of Paul. We find it also in Romans 15:30, 1 Corinthians 2:2–5, 14–16; 6:11,17,19,20; 12:3–6; 2 Corinthians 1:21, 22; 3:3; 13:14; Galatians 3:1–11; 4:6; Ephesians 2:18,20–22; 3:14–16; 4:4–6; Philippians 3:3; Colossians 1:6–8; 2 Thessalonians 2:13–14; Titus 3:4–6; Hebrews 10:29; 1 Peter 1:2; Jude 20, 21; Revelation 1:4b–5.

Endnotes

1. An excellent book on this topic is Wainwright, A.W., *The Trinity in the New Testament* (SPCK, 1962).
2. The Authorised Version of Acts 20:28 and 1 Timothy 3:16 rests upon inferior manuscripts. There is a similar variant reading in Galatians 2:20 ('the faith of God and Christ . . .') which is interesting but probably not original.
3. The Greek word means 'into' rather than 'in'. See Carson, D.A., Matthew, in *The Expositor's Bible Commentary*, 8 (Zondervan, 1984), p. 597. 'In' and 'into' are clearly distinguished in Matthew's Gospel.

PART FOUR:
KNOWING GOD BY NAME

ELEVEN

A Strong Tower

In our meditating on how we experience God, the next matter is that of the name and the names of God. There is a difference between the name of God and the names of God. The Bible has a lot to say about the name of God, and it also gives God particular names and titles.

What is the name of God? J.A. Motyer has three points in this connection which are helpful to us. 'The name is the person. . . . The name is the person revealed. . . . The name is the person actively present'.[1] God can be spoken of as 'the name'. Leviticus 24:11 speaks of someone who 'blasphemed the name'. More than anything and anyone in the universe God is 'the name'. He is the one whose description and character and self-revelation are more amazing, more full, more splendid than any other.

God's name is his character. His name is great because his character has been revealed as great (Ps. 76:1; Jer. 10:6). His name is his revealed faithfulness, righteousness, holiness, goodness. The name of the LORD means 'the LORD as he reveals himself', 'the LORD in the character that he has revealed himself as having'. It is the living personality of God as actively present, as being there to act in mercy and in judgment. Being there to be himself. When Moses says 'I know you by name' (Exod. 33:12) it means that he has experienced God. God has revealed his character to Moses. 'I know you by character; I know what you are like'.

When the psalm writer says, 'I will declare your name' (Ps. 22:22) he means that he will tell everyone what God is like. The name is the character of God. 'Your name is great in might' (Jer. 10:6) means that God has revealed himself as being great in might. Psalm 76:1, 'God is known . . . his name is great in Israel'. This means that God has revealed his character in Israel. When Jesus said, 'I have manifested your name' it is a way of saying that he has revealed what God is like (John 17:6). The disciples have seen what God is like in Jesus. They know what God is like, through Jesus.

We can 'call upon the name of the Lord' (Gen. 4:17). This is not simply to say the syllables of a label, but it is to call upon his character. It is to ask him to be what he is, to act in terms of what he is known to be. The human race began early to 'call upon the name of the Lord' in this way (Gen. 4:26). Abraham called upon God in worship and petition (Gen. 12:8; 13:4; 21:33). In a time of trouble Hagar did the same (Gen. 16:13). She was in trouble and called upon God to act in his mercy. So did Isaac (Gen. 26:25).

When we pray we ask his mercy and his blessings 'for his name's sake'. This means 'because of his mercy rather than because of what we are' (see 1 Sam. 12:22; Ezek. 20:44) or 'because of what he has revealed himself to be as a God of mercy' (see Ps. 23:3; 25:11; Jer. 14:7, where the context always stresses God's mercy over against man's unworthiness). In the New Testament this idea is heightened because the mercy of God has been revealed and highlighted in Jesus as never before. To pray 'in Jesus' name' must in the light of the Old Testament usage mean to pray depending on God's mercy as revealed to us in Jesus. It is to plead his atoning blood and to deliberately reject the idea of approaching God in our own righteousness. When God does something, he acts out of regard to his character. The glory of God's name is revealed (Ps. 79:9) and the nations get a true view of God (Ps. 79:10). God chastens Israel in order to act in character (Ezek. 36:21), 'out of concern for his holy name'. When he restores Israel it will not be because Israel is deserving but because he is revealing his holy mercy. 'It is not for your sake . . . but for the sake of my holy name . . . I will show the holiness of my great name' (Ezek. 36:21–23). God acts to express what he is. He will not do anything which is un-God-like. So the phrase 'for your name's sake' means 'because of what you are, because of what you have promised to do'. When we pray 'for the sake of God's name', it means we pray he will reveal himself.

To act in the name of God is to act conscious that God is with us acting in his known character. We pray in Jesus' name, i.e. backed by his character, his authority, his will, his blood. We baptize in the name of Jesus, that is, conscious that where faith is expressed, God is likely to be acting in blessing. To prophesy in his name is to speak with his words and his authority (Matt. 7:22). To receive a child in Jesus' name is to receive a child because this is what Jesus would do and we do the same with his authority and blessing (Matt. 18:5). We also are called upon to 'suffer for the sake of the name' (Matt. 10:22). It means when we live in his power we shall be treated as he was treated.

To be gathered in his name is to assemble with the consciousness that we are under his authority and promised blessing (Matt. 18:20). We may minister 'in the name of the Lord' (Matt. 21:9; 23:39) genuinely or falsely (Matt. 24:5). We cast out demons in Jesus' name (Mark 9:38).

The Bible has a lot to say about the treatment of God's name. We are told that his name can be blasphemed (Isa. 52:5) or polluted (Jer. 34:16). That is, we may damage God's reputation. But we are also told that people can love God's name (Ps. 5:11) or praise his name (Joel 2:26) or walk in his name (Mic. 4:5) – act upon the way we know he is. We can think upon his name (Mal. 3:16) or wait upon his name (Ps. 52:9) or give thanks to his name (Ps. 54:6, RSV). We can fear his name (Mal. 4:2) and call upon his name (Ps. 99:6) and proclaim his name (Isa. 12:4, RSV) and we can bless his name (Ps. 145:1, 2).

We must take care what we do with God's name. We must not neglect what God is like. We must not have a low view of his character. We must praise his name – see who he is. We must not misuse his name (Exod. 20:7; Lev. 18:21; 19:12; 24:11).

Sometimes the Bible speaks of the 'dwelling-place' of God's name. This refers to the place where God causes his character to shine out in some way. God's name was in Jerusalem. This means that he specially revealed his character there in the temple. Inside the temple was the holy of holies and the glory of God shone in that place. It was the very direct, revealed presence of God. The Bible says that God's name was there. God recorded his name in Israel (Exod. 20:24) and caused it to dwell among them (Deut. 16:11; 12:5), especially in the temple (2 Sam. 7:13) where he 'dwells' (2 Chr. 20:9; 33:4).

By his name he saves (Ps. 54:1). Because of his name he cannot leave Israel (1 Sam. 12:22; Isa. 48:9, 11; Ps. 31:3; 23:3; 143:11ff).

We are to be gripped by the conviction concerning what God is like. We must be preoccupied with him. The world is secular in many places. It does not take God into account. We are to be the very opposite: aware of God, knowing that God is there, revering his name.

The name of the Lord is great (Ezek. 36:23), holy (Ezek. 36:20), terrible (Ps. 111:9). It is a high tower (Ps. 18:2), a strong tower (Prov. 18:10).

We call upon the name of the LORD; we proclaim his name; we exalt his name; we make his name known; we confess his name, fear his name, magnify his name, cherish his name, seek his name, sanctify his name (Gen. 4:26; 12:2; Exod. 9:16; Deut. 28:58; I Ki. 8:33; Ps. 5:11; 34:3; 52:9; 83:16; 122:4; Isa. 26:8; Matt. 6:9; John 12:28).

The Christian learns to praise God's name and live in the strength of God's name. The name of the LORD is a strong tower into which the righteous run to be safe (Prov. 18:10). The Christian learns to live on what God is like, what he has been experienced to be, and upon what he has promised he will be to us. When the Christian is puzzled, is in trouble, is criticized or slandered, he turns to God's name. God has revealed himself as one who is merciful, powerful, kindly, all-powerful. He trusts in this revelation of God. 'Those that know your name' – says Psalm 9:10 – 'shall put their trust in you. For you, Lord, have not forsaken those that seek you'.

Endnote

1. Article 'Name' in *New Bible Dictionary* (IVP, 1965), pp. 862–863. The entire article should be consulted. Bavinck, H., *The Doctrine of God* (Eerdmans, 1955), ch. 3, also has excellent material on this theme.

TWELVE

The Word 'God'

Now we think not of the name of God but of the particular phrases and words that are used to describe God.

In English we have the words 'God' and 'Lord'. In the Old Testament there are many words, names and compound phrases referring to God. Let me begin by listing some of them (without explanation) and then we can consider their meanings. (1) There are three Hebrew words for God ('el, 'elohim and 'eloah), and one Greek word for God (theos). (2) The greatest of God's names – and the word which really is God's personal name – is Yahweh. (3) We have also the terms, 'adon and 'adonai, both of which mean 'lord' or 'sovereign'. Then there are (4) five compound names with the word 'el: 'El Shaddai, 'El 'Elyon, 'El 'Olam, 'El Ro'i, 'El Bethel, (5) Yahweh-who-is-Hosts or Yahweh-God-who-is-Hosts, and a string of names or descriptive titles which use the word Yahweh: Yahweh-'Elohim, Yah, 'Adonai-Yahweh-Sebaoth, Yah-Yahweh, Yah-'Elohim, and several Yahweh titles: Yahweh Yireh, Yahweh Raphah, Yahweh Nissi, Yahweh Kanna, Yahweh Mekaddeskum, Yahweh Shalom, Yahweh Shapat, Yahweh 'Elyon, Yahweh Ra'ah, Yahweh Hosen, Yahweh Gibbor, Yahweh Tsidekenu, Yahweh Shammah. There is also the descriptive title, 'the Holy One' or 'the Holy One of Israel'.

Let us begin with the three Hebrew words for God ('el, 'elohim, 'eloah). They are more or less interchangeable. They are not names but plain and ordinary words meaning God. In Greek the word is theos which again is an ordinary word meaning God. These words are not titles. In the Bible even unbelievers, non-Israelites and non-Christians, and members of the various world religions use the word God. Even people who do not believe in the God of the Bible will use the word God. Everyone knows that God is there. So it is used by many religions and faiths.

The commonest word is *'elohim*, God. It comes 2570 times in the Old Testament.[1] In the Bible it is associated with creation and universal authority. 'In the beginning God (*'elohim*) created the heavens and the earth' (Gen. 1:1). The word reminds us of God being the creator. It speaks of his power, his presence, his being there. The word *'elohim* – God – comes 33 times in Genesis 1:1–2:3. It speaks again and again of God's work as creator. It is God who speaks, creates, gives character to the different parts of the world, and brings things into the order and arrangement that he wants. The word is actually a plural word and can sometimes mean gods, and yet it generally has a singular meaning. The idea is that all the possible divine powers are concentrated in one God. He is everything that can claim to be divine, all in the one God.

The word God is used in descriptive phrases like 'a jealous God' (Deut. 4:2; 5:9; 6:15; Josh. 24:19), 'Yahweh, Yahweh God, compassionate and gracious, slow to anger . . .' (Exod. 34:6), 'a merciful God' (Deut. 4:31), 'the faithful God' (Deut. 7:9; see also 32:4), 'a great and awesome God' (Deut. 7:21), 'a great God and mighty' (Deut. 10:17), 'the living God' (Josh. 3:10), 'a God of knowledge' (1 Sam. 2:3), a 'gracious and merciful God . . . our God, the great, the mighty, and the awe-inspiring God, who keeps covenant and loving kindness' (Neh. 9:31, 32). Similar descriptions are found throughout the Old Testament.[2]

Another word for God is the word *'el*. It is simply a variant of *'elohim* but tends to be used in descriptions of God, and situations where pagans are talking or are being addressed. It is also much used in combinations, as we shall see below. It is used in poetry as a variant of *'elohim*.

On its own it occurs in Genesis 35:1, 3; 46:3; 49:25; Exodus 15:2; 20:5; Numbers 12:13; Deuteronomy 32:18; 2 Samuel 22:31, 32, 33, 48; 23:5; often in the book of Job (e.g. 5:8; 8:3, 5, 13, 20; and elsewhere), often in the psalms (Ps. 5:4; 7:11 and elsewhere), sometimes in the prophets (Isa. 5:16; 8:10, and elsewhere). Balaam used it several times in his poetic oracles to a pagan king (Num. 23:8, 19, 22, 23; 24:4, 8, 16, 23). El was a very common word outside Israel. This is why David can say 'Who is El besides Yahweh?' (2 Sam. 22:32). When we use the word God on its own we mean the creator, the one that everyone knows about in his or her heart, the one who is great and is king over the universe.

Another variant of the same word is *'eloah*. This is the same word as *'elohim* but it is singular in structure whereas technically *'elohim* is a plural word with a singular meaning. *'eloah* is used in Nehemiah 9:17, 'You are a God ready to pardon . . .' and elsewhere especially in the book of Job (Job 3:4, 23; 4:9, 17; 5:17; and often afterwards) and in the book of Psalms (Ps. 18:31; 50:22, and so on), and in the works of the prophets. *'eloah* is the same word as *'elohim* but emphasizes singularity. It means 'the one God' (Deut. 32:15; Dan. 2:11).

'God' appears in the phrase 'walk with God' in Genesis 5:22, 24. Perhaps the emphasis is on the great privilege of walking with one's creator.

In the Greek New Testament, *theos* (God) has the same meaning. It picks up its meaning not from Greek culture but from the Greek translation of the Old Testament. So it carries the ideas of the Old Testament words for God. In the New Testament the word God is often used when stressing the uniqueness of God ('the only true God', John 17:3; 'No idol is anything. . . . There is no God but one' I Cor. 8:4). He is the creator of everything (see 1 Cor. 8:6); over everything (Eph. 4:6; 1 Cor. 12:6), gives life and existence to everything (Acts 17:25, 28, 27). He is personal; he acts freely and powerfully in our world; he relates to men and women through Jesus. Again the New Testament like the Old Testament uses the word God in descriptive phrases, like 'the eternal God' (Rom. 16:26), the 'invisible God' (Rom. 1:20), the 'blessed God' (1 Tim. 1:17), the 'incorruptible God' (Rom. 1:23), and so on.[3]

One point of interest is that God in the New Testament nearly always refers to God the Father. When the New Testament says we are 'children of God' it means were we are children of God the Father. It does not mean that we are the children of Jesus or children of the Holy Spirit or children of the Father, the Son and the Holy Spirit. We are children of the Father! When we have reference to Jesus as the Son of God or to the Spirit of God, the word God refers to the Father. There is no verse of Scripture in which 'God' means the Father, the Son and the Spirit considered as one. In texts which refer to the three persons,[4] God always refers to the Father.

There is a popular mistake that arises from the fact that all sorts of religions and philosophies use the same word God for what they believe in. 'Surely', it is often said, 'we all believe in God'. There is only one God. All religions use the word 'God', so they are all talking about the same being even though they might have slightly different ideas. 'We all believe in God!' they say.

No! This is not true at all. The fact that all religions use the word God, does not at all mean they are all believing in one and the same God. The apostle Paul was quite clear that other gods beside the God and Father of our Lord Jesus Christ are idols. Jesus claimed that he alone was the way to God (John 14:6) and that the only God was the God approached through him. He is 'the only true God' (John 17:3). 'No idol is anything. . . . There is no God but one', said Paul and he was quite clear that the one and only God is the Father of Jesus.

The cause of the confusion is that many religions use the word God for what they believe in, but what they believe in is in each case fairly distinctive. If the God of Hinduism is God, all other gods are not God because they are different. If the God of Islam is God, all other gods are not God because they are different. And if the God and Father of our Lord Jesus Christ is the one and only God, then all other so-called gods are not gods at all because they are different from the one who is God!

For example, the God of Hinduism, the impersonal 'it' that is unreachable and unlovable and is over and above the countless deities of Hinduism, is a whole universe away from the God and Father of our Lord Jesus Christ. Hinduism and the Christian faith may both use the word God but only the abysmally ignorant could dream that they worship the same God.

God is a general word which millions of people use. The biblical teaching is that most people's idea of God has been grossly corrupted. They 'changed the glory of the incorruptible God', said Paul about the Roman Empire, and something similar could be said about the entire human race and every culture. The Bible uses the word God because the biblical writers are aware that everyone has a sense that God is there and that he is real.

Yet the Bible goes on to add something additional: 'Who is God besides Yahweh?' (2 Sam. 22:32). The answer is: no one and nothing. The only God is the God and Father of our Lord Jesus Christ.

Endnotes

1. See *TDOT* (*Theological Dictionary of the Old Testament*. Botterweck, G.J. & Ringren, H. (eds), (Eerdmans), 1, p. 272.
2. *TDOT*, 1, p. 275, has a list of them. The whole article is worth reading.
3. Karl Rahner's article, 'Theos in the New Testament', in *Theological Investigations*, 1 (Darton, Longman & Todd, 1974) is full of interesting information along these lines.
4. Matt. 28:19, Luke 24:49; John 14:16, 17, 26; 15:26; 16:7–11, 12–15; Acts 2:32–33, 38–39; 5:31–32; 7:55–56; 10:38; 11:15–17; Rom. 5:1–5; 8:9–11; 14:17–18; 15:15–16, 30; 1 Cor. 2:6–16; 6:11, 15–20; 12:3. 4–6; 2 Cor. 1:21–22; 13:13; Gal. 4:4–6; Eph. 1:13–14, 17; 2:18–22; 3:14–19; 4:4–6; 5:15–20; 2 Thess. 2:13; Titus 3:4–11; Heb. 2:2–4; 10:29–31; 1 Pet. 1:1–2; 2:4–5; 4:14; 1 John 3:23–24; 4:11–16; 5:5–8; Jude 20–21.

THIRTEEN

The God who Redeems by the Blood of a Lamb

In biblical times names generally had meanings. When Abram was told he would be the father of many nations he was given the name Abraham (father of a multitude). Simon the disciple of Jesus was given the name Peter (rock), and so on. Names generally had a meaning. In English, names are often just labels, but in many cultures names have meanings and it was that way in Bible times. So the 'name of God' is his description, and the actual names and titles used for God tell us a lot about him. Knowing God involves leaning on what we know him to be. We do not lean upon some theory, or some idea. God is alive. We trust him and experience him as the living God. His names tell us who he is and what he is like. We live on the real God, the God who is there.

We come now to consider the word Lord There are two words in the Old Testament generally translated lord. One of them is a name, often translated Yahweh or Jehovah. The other one – Adonai – is not actually a name; it is simply a word meaning king or master.

Let us first consider LORD as a translation of Yahweh. It is really and genuinely a name, and is the greatest name for God. It occurs over six thousand times in the Hebrew Old Testament. Yahweh is almost certainly the right way to spell it, although it has become a tradition to spell it as Jehovah. In many English Bible translations it is translated as 'the LORD', with capital O, capital R and capital D, as well as a capital L. (Lord is a different word from LORD as we have seen).

What happened was this. The Jews felt that they should not pronounce the holy name, Yahweh. Hebrew writing generally had no vowels in it. When the Jew saw the word YHWH he did not read it as 'Yahweh'; instead he said 'Lord' (Adonai). To make sure that 'Adonai' was said and not 'Yahweh', the later medieval Jews wrote 'Yehowah' – which is an impossible Hebrew word. This is where the word Jehovah comes from. It is a combination of the consonants of YHWH plus the e, o, and a, taken from the word Adonai (or Edonai). They also sometimes wrote it as Yehowih (an equally impossible form) which has the e, o, and i of Elohim (God), and prompted the reader to use the word God. The two impossible forms, Yehowah(??) and Yehowih(??) (deliberately misspelt to inform the reader he should read Adonai or Elohim) both occur in the Hebrew of Obadiah, verse 1. However the pronunciation was Yahweh. It can be seen in words like Hallelujah (Praise Yahweh), where the last three letters, – yah, are a short form of Yahweh.

More important than its exact spelling is the significance of the name. Yahweh is God's name. It was a name explained by God himself at the time of the Exodus. At this particular time God 'got himself a name'. Before that time the name Yahweh had been known but its meaning and significance were not known. Only from the events of the Exodus, when the Israelites were delivered from Egyptian bondage, does it become clear what God's inner name and nature mean. As Exodus 6:2–3 puts it, 'I appeared to Abraham, Isaac and Jacob in the character of El Shaddai, but in the character of my name Yahweh I did not make myself known to them'.

When Moses was summoned to be the leader and mediator of a new phase of God's salvation he asked the question, 'What does your name mean?'[1]. The reply is given 'I am who I am', or later in the same verse, simply 'I am' (Exod. 3:14). The name Yahweh is clearly related to this revelation of the divine name. It is a very archaic form of the Hebrew word for 'He is'. In later Hebrew it would have been Yihyeh but in early proto-Semitic the form of 'He is' was Yahweh.[2] Although the linguistics of the matter is complicated, the main point is clear and indisputable. Yahweh is shorthand for 'I am that I am'.

Moses was told to go and deliver Israel (Exodus). Moses said:

'What if they ask me about your name?'. God answered and said his name was 'I AM THAT I AM'. The word Yahweh means 'He is'. It is linked with the verb 'to be'. God's name is I AM THAT I AM, or (a shorter form) I AM, or (a one-word version) YAHWEH.

God reveals his name: I AM THAT I AM, shortened to I AM, further shortened to HE IS. In the book of Exodus the name is progressively shortened. First we have the fullest form (Exod. 3:14), then a slightly shorter form, then simply Yahweh (LORD).

What does it mean? It means that in what God would do at the time of the Exodus, he would reveal himself. The event would reveal God's nature. What would happen expresses what he is in his character. The events of the Exodus reveal what God really is. God says: 'You see what I am now – that is what I am all the time. That is my name'. God revealed himself. He got a meaning for that name Yahweh.

What then is the significance of 'I am that I am' or Yahweh? God's explanation of his name referred Moses to what was just about to happen. It refers to events, not to anything metaphysical (such as immutability or self-existence). 'Look at what I am about to do', says God in effect. 'Look at me in action; I am about to get myself a name' (Neh. 9:10).

The name 'I am that I am' refers to history. It is not what God is in himself. It is not a prediction. But it refers to what God will show himself to be. 'When you see me in action', says God, 'you see what I am. What I am about to show myself as being in these coming events – that is what I am'. We are not like the philosophers, who were concerned about God's unchangeability. We are to think of how God has revealed himself in action.

After the events of the Exodus, the Old Testament looks back to the Exodus as the occasion when meaning was given to the name Yahweh. 'I am Yahweh your God, who brought you out of the land of Egypt' begins the Ten Commandments (Exod. 20:2). Centuries later the people of Israel remind themselves that the name Yahweh was given its definitive content during the Exodus: 'You saw the affliction of our fathers in Egypt . . . And you made for yourself a name as it is this day' (Neh. 9:9, 10).

To put it simply we can say Yahweh means, 'The God who redeems by the blood of a lamb'. He is the God of the Exodus.

He is the Holy One who revealed himself in blazing fire without having the need to consume any fuel in the process (Exod. 3:2). He is the God of self-sufficient and self-existent holiness. He is the God who cannot be lightly approached (Exod. 3:4–5), the God who cannot be looked upon (Exod. 3:6). He is the God who becomes angry with the stubbornness of Moses (Exod. 4:14, 24) and who acts in indignation against sin (Exod. 4:23; 7:4; 12:12). He is the God who makes a distinction between his people and Egypt (Exod. 11:7), who redeems some with an outstretched hand (Exod. 6:6) but who leaves others to be hardened in their sins (Exod. 4:21).

He is the God of grace, who chooses those who can scarcely believe themselves chosen (Exod. 3:10, 11), who knows the end from the beginning because he will bring his plan to pass (Exod. 3:18–21). He is one who takes a people for himself (Exod. 6:7), in his own time and in his own way, who calls slaves in Egypt 'my people' (Exod. 3:10), who is ever-present with his servants (Exod. 3:12), and who demands to be worshipped (Exod. 3:12).

He is the God who delivers from judgment 'by the blood of the lamb', who executes his wrath but at the same time provides a substitute for his people, whom he has already chosen (Exod. 12:12–13, 23), who demands that his people set out for a 'promised land' (Exod. 12:25) with the utmost urgency (Exod. 12:34), with himself 'going before them' (Exod. 13:21), 'in his loving-kindness leading those whom He has redeemed, (Exod. 15:13). He is the God who is his people's 'strength and song' (Exod. 15:2) and their 'salvation' (Exod. 15:2), whose right hand is 'majestic in power' (Exod. 15:6), who is 'majestic in holiness, awesome in praises, working wonders' (Exod. 15:11). 'Yahweh' is his name (Exod. 15:3); and this is his name 'for ever' and his 'memorial-name to all generations' (Exod. 3:15). May he 'reign for ever and ever' (Exod. 15:18)!

Never should the name Yahweh be used unless it contains this Exodus-content. This is the background to the six thousand and more uses of this term throughout the Old Testament.

We can summarize the teaching in three points:

1. Our God, Yahweh, is the God who redeems a people by the blood of the lamb. When God was saving Israel, he used blood. By means of the blood the people were saved, were freed

from bondage, and became God's people. This is the meaning of the term Yahweh: God who redeems by the blood of the lamb.

2. Our God, Yahweh, is the God who steps into the lives of those who are in bondage, and brings them release.

3. Our God, Yahweh, is the God who chooses a people for himself. God stepped into the life of Moses and chose a people for himself. He chose no other nation. Yahweh means the God who takes a people and becomes their God.

Endnotes

1. Not 'What is your name?' which in classical Hebrew would be *mi semeka*. The phrase here is *mah shemeka* which enquires after significance. See Judg. 13:17 and Motyer J.A., *The Revelation of the Divine Name* (Tyndale).
2. Those who know Hebrew will have to forgive my simplified account of a complicated subject. I can refer them to Albrektson, B., On the Syntax of ['hyh 'shr 'hyh] in Exodus 3:14, in *Words and Meanings* (CUP, 1968), pp. 15–28.

FOURTEEN

Adonai; El Shaddai

There is a second word which is generally translated lord and that is the word, Adonai, which means king or sovereign. The word lord in the English language has the idea of power of authority. The same thing is true of the Hebrew word. It is a word linked with kingship.

There is an example of this in Isaiah 6. 'In the year that king Uzziah died I saw the Lord' (Isa. 6:1). The word there is not Yahweh but Adonai. It means king or master or sovereign. So Isaiah says: In the year that king Uzziah died I saw God as king. In the year in which one king died I saw another king. In the year the earthly king died I saw the heavenly king. Later he says, 'My eyes have seen the King' (Isa. 6:5).

Yahweh is a different word and is a genuine name. Nehemiah 9:10 refers to the time of the Exodus when it says, 'You made a name for yourself as it is at this day'. God revealed the kind of God he was. He revealed himself in these historical events.

Adonai is different. It means the sovereign one. Sometimes you get the two names together. In Isaiah 7:7 the two words for lord are side by side. It speaks of God as 'Lord LORD' but with two different Hebrew words. The New International Version has 'sovereign LORD'. The two words are alongside one another, one meaning lord, king, master, and the other meaning the God who redeems by the blood of a lamb.

Something similar happens in Isaiah 6 where we have the two words meaning Lord in the same chapter. First Isaiah says, 'I saw the Lord', and then goes on to talk about the 'LORD of hosts'. You can tell the difference in some Bibles because Yahweh is translated as LORD wholly in capital letters (LORD) but the other word has only a capital L (Lord). In Isaiah 6 and 7:7 you can see both Lord and LORD.

We may contrast also the word God and the name Yahweh. It is often illuminating to see how the biblical writers use them differently at times. Consider for example the use of the words God and Yahweh in Genesis 1–4. In the section about creation (1:1–2:3) only the word God is used (34 times). A new section starts in 2:4. This will be not so much about creation as about man and God's love of man. So 2:4–3:1 speaks of 'Yahweh God' 12 times, using both words). When the woman speaks to Satan she says 'Has God said . . .?', using only the word God (3:1; see also 3:5). God is not Yahweh (Redeemer) to the devil.

The narrator of the Genesis-story continues to use the words Yahweh God in 3:8–23 (8 times). By the end of chapter 3 it is quite clear that God and Yahweh are the same person. The term Yahweh God has been used 20 times. From that point on the narrator can simply use the word Yahweh. It is the name of God and by this stage of the narrative the reader is thoroughly aware that God and Yahweh refer to one and the same God. From Genesis 4 onwards both God and Yahweh are used. When God's relationship with man is emphasized Yahweh tends to be the word (4:1–16, 9 times; and 5:29). Yahweh is used when worship is the theme (4:26). God is used in 4:25 (similar to 4:1 where Yahweh was used). When creation is mentioned God is the word used (5:1). Also when the 'image of God' is being spoken of, the word God is used (Gen. 5:1). The Bible does not speak of the image of Yahweh in this connection. Man is Godlike in connection with God the Creator, more than in connection with God the Redeemer, that is, in the image of God more than the image of Yahweh.

We have now considered the common words for God (*'el, 'elohim, 'eloah, theos*) and a title that God has (Adonai) and God's name (Yahweh). Now we must take a look at compound names. First, consider the compound names using the word God (El). The greatest of the compound names which have the word God (El) in them is El Shaddai. It was the main name for God used by Abraham, Isaac, Jacob and Joseph. After the time of Moses, when God 'got himself a name', Yahweh became the main name of God, but before that time, between Abraham and Moses the most important name for God was El Shaddai. Exodus 6:2 makes the point that it was the main name used before the days of the Exodus.

The meaning of the actual syllables Shaddai is totally unknown. No one knows its etymology, that is, its derivation. The way to study the meaning of El Shaddai is not to study its etymology (which leads to a dead-end) but to study its usage. When this is done it is clear that the name has the meaning of 'The God who is powerful to act when we are in a desperate situation'. When its usage is studied we find it was always used, in patriarchal times when its meaning was established, in situations where God's people are specially needy. It means 'the God who is Almighty on behalf of the helpless'.

In Genesis 17:1, Abraham has been promised a son, but the son has not been born. Now Abraham is old. The name is used in a situation of desperate need. In Genesis 28:3, Jacob was in bad trouble and was running away from home. In this desperate situation El Shaddai is the one who can bless.

Again in Genesis 35:11 we find a patriarch in trouble. He again is in a crisis situation about to meet his brother who had threatened to kill him.

In Genesis 43:14, Jacob is having to release Benjamin. He has already lost Joseph (or so he thinks). Now it seems he will lose Benjamin. So he says 'May El Shaddai show you mercy'.

In Genesis 48:3, Jacob is on his deathbed and refers to the time when he was in such a terrible situation and El Shaddai appeared to him.

In Genesis 49:25, Jacob is giving his farewell blessing. He talks of Joseph (v.23) and refers to the time when he had been attacked by the family and by Potiphar's wife. But 'El Shaddai . . . blesses you'.

Thus it can be seen that there is a consistent pattern in the use of El Shaddai. It means 'The God who is powerful to act when his people are in a desperate situation' or (as Alec Motyer once put it), 'The God who takes you from the dungeon to the throne in one step'.

These marvellous names of God tell us of what God is like. When you look into the heart of God you find he lives up to his name. He releases us from our sins by the blood of Jesus. He comes to our aid when we are in distress. It is possible to experience God for what he is. He will live up to his name for you. If you have trusted Jesus you have already discovered him as Yahweh. He has already proved himself to you as the God who has redeemed you by the blood of Jesus, the Lamb of God. You can also be sure that he will be El Shaddai to you. You can utterly trust him to be the God who brings you from the dungeon to the throne. There is no need for you to live in fearfulness or in panic. He will never let you down. He is Yahweh; he is El Shaddai and he will stay that way for ever.

FIFTEEN
God Most High

There are four more compound names with the word 'El: 'El 'Elyon, 'El Ro'i, 'El 'Olam, 'El Bethel. (We can leave aside 'El 'Elohe Yisrael in Genesis 32:20 because it is the name of an altar, not a name of God. It means God, the God of Israel. In this verse Israel is the person, Jacob, not the nation of Israel).

'El 'Elyon comes in Genesis 14 where we have the story of how Abraham meets a high priest of God, Melchizedek. His name has a meaning. Melchi-zedek means king of righteousness. The order of his priesthood was unique. He was king of peace, in that he ruled in a city known for peace, and he was king of righteousness in his own person. Melchizedek comes out to meet Abraham bringing bread to build up his strength, and refreshing dilute wine. Melchizedek prays for Abraham. Then he points Abraham to God's greatness by using the name for God, El Elyon, God Most High. This is the name that the people of Salem use for God. It is used three times in Genesis 14:18, 19, 20 and a fourth time in Abraham's words, 'Yahweh God Most High', in 14:22.

Melchizedek and his people were conscious that there were other spiritual beings that claimed to be gods or sons of the gods, but they are not God in the full sense of the term. El Elyon, God Most High, expressed the thought that the God of Melchizedek is the one and only God above all other claimants to deity. The idea of being above also expresses the notion of control. The God of Melchizedek is the Lord; he is over everything. It has the idea of knowledge. When you are at a high point you see in one sweep everything that is below.

We note that when Abraham speaks next he uses the phrase 'Yahweh, God Most High' (Gen. 14:22). He brings the two names

together! Abraham is making it clear Yahweh and El Elyon and
the same one-and-only God.

We need to see God as God Most High. He is above every
other power, every form of opposition. Everything else is subject
to him. When he is for us, nothing can be against us.

El Roi, 'the God who sees', is found in Genesis 16:13–14. Sarai
was feeling a failure. In her feeling of failure she made a big
mistake. In those days, it was possible for a man with a childless
wife to make use of a slave-girl in order to produce a child. In
such a situation the childless wife took the child as her own and
the true mother had no rights in the matter. So Sarai suggests
that the pagan custom be followed and that Abraham should get
a child through Hagar. She was acting without sense, without
foresight, without guidance, without assurance. She could only
say 'it may be' (16:2).

Hagar had been a slave-girl for many years. To sleep with
Abraham meant that she was being taken as a subordinate wife
(16:3). For a slave-girl it was a kind of promotion! She becomes
pregnant. But then she starts acting with scorn towards Sarai.
What a mess it was! Everyone was making big mistakes. It all
leads to bitterness. Sarai resents being treated in the way that
she is. It leads to irresponsibility on the part of Abraham. 'Do to
her what you like' (16:6), he says. Yet this leads to cruelty by
Sarai and suffering for Hagar. Sarai treats Hagar harshly and
Hagar runs away heading for Egypt (16:6b).

But where sin abounds, grace abounds all the more. God
shows mercy when everyone else is showing their foolishness.
God sought Hagar (16:7). The 'angel of Yahweh' is God himself,
appearing in visible form. 'No one has seen God at any time'
(John 1:18), but there was something visible representing God.
The 'angel of Yahweh' speaks so kindly that Hagar is led to trust
him with her story. She makes no attempt to disguise who she
is and what has happened to her. God told her what to do (16:9).
Hagar is told that she should return and submit to Sarai. God
gave promises concerning her child. The true 'seed of Abram'
will be Sarai's son. Yet the promise to Hagar is close to what she
had hoped would come to her as Abraham's wife. It echoes the
promises of a numerous seed that God had given to Abraham.
She will have a son (16:11). He will be a highly individualistic

person living where he likes and doing what he likes, and so clashing with everyone (16:12).

It is in this context that she starts using a new name for God. Just as Abraham had come to appreciate God as El Elyon (14:22), so now Hagar comes to appreciate God as El Roi (God of seeing) because, as she said, 'Truly here in this place I have seen him who looks after me' (16:13).

El Roi is the God who sees. He sees our mistakes and yet treats them with mercy. He sees our sufferings and in his appointed time has plans to bring them to an end. In the midst of jealousy, cruelty, irresponsibility, impatience, and abundant sinfulness, God's grace stepped into the life of the most despised slave-girl, and showed her his kindliness. From that point on she would never forget what had happened to her. She now knew God as the one who had been caring for her all along. Sin was multiplying but grace was multiplying all the more. God is the God who sees.

In Genesis 21:22–34 we have another story which introduces us to El Olam. Abraham had dug wells in an area which Abimelech the Philistine ruler regarded as his. Then Abimelech's servants had seized the wells. They regarded him as an alien from Haran who had no right to claim the use of any land, not even water-wells! But suddenly there is a change. At the celebration of the weaning of Isaac, Abimelech the Philistine leader and Phicol the commander of his army were present as visitors and approached Abraham with a request (21:22a). They were so impressed with the obvious success of Abraham (21:22b) that they wanted to enter into a covenant-relationship with him. They ask Abraham to swear an oath. Abraham joins in the oath as they wish but he has a request. He wants the use of his water-wells! The request is accepted (21:31), and the men swear an oath there. Abraham is making some steps towards getting the promises of God fulfilled. He had been promised land, and now some leading men of the land of Canaan recognize that Abraham has had a certain amount of success in the land of Canaan. They talk about 'the country where you are living as an alien'. Yet they recognize that Abraham is being blessed by his God. So they accept his residence in the land and they leave him with the use of the water-wells. Abraham now uses a new name for God, El Olam, the Everlasting God. Abraham thinks of the distant future. Will the land that he has been promised ever belong to him? Perhaps not, because he is now getting elderly. It seems that he is only getting a few small privileges such as the use of the water-wells he had dug. But – he thinks to himself – God is the Everlasting God. When Abraham has left this world, God will still be there. The promise to him has spoken of a vast nation and of many kings coming from his 'seed'. This must mean that the promise extends out into the vast future ahead of him and ahead of his lifetime. Will Canaan ever belong to his seed? Yes! God is El Olam – the everlasting God. His plans come about slowly, but God is over and above the ages of time. He looks back and he looks ahead with perfect knowledge of what his plans are and what he is going to do.

'El Bethel is the name that is associated with Jacob. We know him from the Bible as a tricky, grasping character. He got himself into bad trouble because of his devious ways. He created a bad relationship with his brother and so violent was the aggressiveness between them, Jacob was in danger of being killed. His mother sent him back to stay with his uncle Laban in faraway Haran.

As he was on his way to Haran God met him. God – as with all the other patriarchs – stepped into his life when he was desperate. He had got himself into bad trouble because of his own twisted personality and deceitful ways. He had a dream and saw the angels of God coming down to care for him. It was a picture of a staircase, but the staircase was not for him to climb up but for the angels to come down (Gen. 28:12–19)! He named the place 'Bethel' – 'house of God'. Jacob never forgot this time in his life. Later when God spoke to him again, God said 'I am El Bethel' – the God of Bethel.

El Bethel is a name which helps us when we feel that we have weakness of character, when we have got ourselves into trouble because of our own foolish ways. When the Bible speaks of the 'God of Jacob' (for example, in Ps. 20:1; 46:7, 11; 75:6 and elsewhere) or the 'God of Bethel' it lets us know that God is the God of the crook, the phoney, the twister. God has a habit of coming into the lives of people who have ruined their lives by their own senselessness – but then he rescues them, saves them, stays with them. 'The God of Jacob is our stronghold' (Ps. 46:7, 11). The theme of the names of God is endless. One should get into a habit of noticing how the names of God in the Bible are used. It is often very illuminating and helpful. There are other themes that could be explored but I have said enough to get us going. The Bible speaks of the 'God of Jeshurun' (Deut. 33:26), and of El-Gibbor, 'the Warrior God' (Isa. 9:6; Jer. 32:18–19). It speaks of Elohim-Sebaoth, the God who has 'hosts' of power and strength in him; the Hebrew here means 'God who is hosts', not 'God of hosts' (see Ps. 80:7, 14). The people of Israel once called out and said 'O God, you who are God of the spirits of all flesh . . .' (Num. 16:22). Sometimes people in the Bible just love to heap up a great pile of names for God. In Joshua 22:22 people speak of 'The Mighty One, God, the LORD, the Mighty One, God, the LORD!' And best of all Jesus is called Immanue-El. God with us (Isa. 7:14).

PART FIVE: EXPERIENCING GOD'S CHARACTER

SIXTEEN

God is Spirit

It is a wonderful thing to think and meditate upon the character of God. One of the great aims of the Christian life is to glorify God. The Bible says that God has saved us to the praise of the glory of his grace. We are to get to see what God is like. When we do that we shall want to praise him for the glory of his grace. We are to get to know what God is like and we are to get to know him personally. Jesus died 'to bring us to God' (I Pet. 3:18).

We come now to think of the way we experience God in the great variety of his character. We begin with some preliminary thoughts:

1. Christians have spent a lot of time discussing how to group these different characteristics of God. I am not very interested in that and shall group them in a very simple way.

2. One must be careful not to think of God as though there were bits and pieces in his nature. God is one. When he acts he acts with the whole of his being. There are no 'parts' of God. Yet it is possible to meditate on different aspects of God's character. Every aspect of God's character holds together with every other aspect. No aspect of his character contradicts any other aspect of his character. His love does not contradict his anger.

3. Is it possible to make a complete list of the characteristics of God? No. Different languages would have different words that could be used. But as we meditate on our experience of God, illumined by God's word, it is possible to see different aspects of his wonderful character.

4. We must be careful not to try to know more than God has told us. We can only know what God has revealed to us. We might like to know more, but all we can do is meditate on the

way in which he has revealed himself to us in Jesus, in our experience of him, and in the Scriptures.

We must remember the mystery of God. He dwells in unapproachable light (1 Tim. 6:16). The nearer you get to God, the more you are dazzled by the brightness of his nature. Psalm 40:5 says, 'No one can compare with you'. God is near to us and yet is great and above us at the same time. He is 'Our Father' but he is also the one 'who is in heaven'. Even when you see his glory in creation you say, 'These are the fringes of his ways. How faint a word we hear of him' (Job 26:14). Zophar in the book of Job asked, 'Can you discover the depths of God?' (Job 11:7). 'Man by wisdom did not know God' (I Cor. 1:21).

5. We must do our meditating in a practical way. If we truly see what God is like it will affect us in the way we live. The Bible always puts things to us practically. When you read the word of God it always shows us the impact it has upon us. Let us see a few examples.

The Old Testament says, 'Be holy because I am holy' (quoted also in I Pet. 1:16). Notice the connection between what God is and what we are to be. We are to live in the light of what God is like. Certain things are to be true of us because of what is true about God. We are to think about him in a very practical way.

Jeremiah puts it the other way round. He says, 'They worshipped vanity and became vanity' (Jer. 2:5). You become like the God you worship. So our view of God is very practical matter. When you draw near to God you become like God in some respects. The greater your fellowship with God the more you will be like him.

Malachi 3:6 says, 'I Yahweh do not change; so you sons of Jacob are not consumed'. The reason why we are not destroyed when we sin is because of what God is like. You see the effect of God's character upon us.

I Peter 1:17 says, 'If you address as Father the one who judges impartially according to each person's work, conduct yourselves with fear during the time here on earth'. One sees the connection between the God whom we address and the way we live. If you see the impartiality of God it will affect the way you live. Our grasp of what God is like will affect us.

We have the same thing in Psalm 139 where the psalmist thinks very practically about the character of God. And the same thing is found in Habakkuk 1. This is the way the character of God is put to us everywhere throughout the pages of Scripture.

Let us begin with a group of characteristics of God that seem to be somehow deeper and very foundational. I call them his basic characteristics. It includes such things as God's spirituality, God's oneness, his independence, his personality, his unchanging character, his power, his being the living God.

First, we shall consider God's spirituality. 'God is spirit'. Consider John 4:20–24 where these words occur. Jesus was speaking to the woman of Samaria, and the conversation led into a discussion concerning worship. Then it led on to something concerning God. 'God is spirit . . .'. Spirit is a form of existence distinct from matter. Angels are 'spirits' (Heb. 1:14). Spiritual beings have no bodies and are invisible. This is the way it is with God.

Part of this is that God is invisible (I Tim. 1:17; 6:15, 16). It might be asked: what about the times in the Old Testament when men saw God? The answer is that they did not see the very being of God himself. The angels were representing God. 'He makes his angels winds and his servants flames of fire' (Heb. 1:7). It was not the very stuff of God appearing. Sometimes God appears as a blazing fire, sometimes as an earthquake. But this is not the very being of God. It is an angel. God himself is invisible. He is the 'blessed God . . . king of kings . . .' and 'alone possesses immortality'. He 'dwells in unapproachable light . . .' and is one 'whom no person has seen or can see'. God is spirit. This does not mean that God is impersonal, an 'it'. God is personal, as we know already and shall see in the Scriptures.

What does it mean to us practically that God is spirit? It affects worship. The material aspects of worship do not matter very much. 'God is spirit.' The woman at the well was very concerned about the physical circumstances of worship. She was preoccupied with mountains where different people worshipped. Jesus replied: 'God is spirit . . .'. What matters is the attitude, the power of the Spirit, submission to God, real fellowship with him. Worship is primarily a spiritual matter. Posture and location come into it a little bit but they are not really the important thing.

What God is concerned about is that our spirit is actually communing with God.

The only way for God to be visible is through Jesus. John 1:18 says 'No one has ever seen God. The only-begotten Son . . . he has declared him'. Jesus is the way to see what God is like. Look at Jesus. He is the image of the invisible God. Through knowing Jesus you see what God is like in human form. God is spirit. Jesus said, 'The Father has borne witness of me. . . . You have neither heard his voice at any time, nor seen his form' (John 5:37). Jesus says: I am the one who tells you what God is like. 'He who has seen me has seen the Father'.

In the second place, consider God's Oneness. God is one, and there is only one God. 'Hear O Israel: the LORD our God, the LORD, is one' (Deut. 6:4; see also Isa. 43:10, 11). I Corinthians 8:5, 6 says, 'There are beings called gods . . . but for us there is but one God, the Father . . . and one Lord Jesus Christ . . .'

It might be asked: what about the doctrine of the Trinity? There is threeness within God, but there is still only God and God is still one. The Trinity does not mean that there are three gods.

What does the one-ness of God mean to us practically?

1. It means that there is only one way of salvation. 'A person is justified by faith apart from works of the law. Or is God the God of Jews only? Is he not the God of Gentiles also? Yes, of Gentiles also, since God is one and he will justify the circumcised by faith and the uncircumcised through faith . . .' (Rom. 3:28–30).

God is one – and so he justifies all people the same way. The reason why there is only one way of salvation is that there is only one God. There is one attitude of God towards sin, one way of dealing with sin. If there were two ways of salvation it would imply that God is double-minded about sin. It is the oneness of God that means – says Paul – that there is only one way of salvation. God is the God of the whole world. All have to be saved in the same way.

This means too that the Christian faith is exclusive. People do not always like this. But there is only one God and he has said what is the way of salvation. So the Christian faith is exclusive. Jesus said, 'I am the way . . . no one comes to the Father except by me'. It is a very exclusive claim. If the Christian faith is right other ways are wrong.

Don't other religions believe in God? They use the word God but that does not mean that they all believe in the God of the Bible. A Muslim does not believe in the God and Father of Jesus. A Hindu does not believe in the God of the Bible. Do they believe in God? Not exactly – they believe in something for which they use the word God – but it is not the God of the Bible, the one and only God. There is only one God and he has revealed himself in one way. We are friendly to other religions but we have to accept the claim of Jesus that he is the only way to the Father. Jesus is the only Son of God. He is the one that claims to be the only God there is. This is the basis of what is the only way of salvation (see Rom. 3:30).

2. It means that we must submit to God as he is. There is no other. 'Before me there was no God formed, neither shall there be any after me . . . . beside me there is no Saviour' (Isa. 43:10). 'Beside me there is no God' (Isa. 43:11).

3. It means that there is no division within God. He is not in conflict with himself. His love and his holiness are aspects of the one God. His love is holy love; his holiness is loving holiness. God is one. There is no internal conflict in God. He does not have a divided mind.

SEVENTEEN
Companionship with God

A third aspect of these basic characteristics of God is what might be called God's independence. God is self-sufficient. He does not depend on anything outside of himself. He does not need to feed on anything. We need him but he does not need us. His relationship to us is one of delight and love not a relationship of need. Acts 17:25 says that he is not ministered to by human hands in the way that idols need to be propped up by human worshippers. He does not need anything from us, although he wants our worship, our love and our obedience. We need him. He gives us life in the first place. He gives us breath to keep us alive. He gives us everything else that comes our way.

God is not in any kind of straitjacket. He existed before all things, and all things exist through him. He depends on nothing; everything depends on him (Rom. 11:36). He does according to his will in the army of heaven, and among the inhabitants of the earth (Dan. 4:35). In his hand people are as clay in the hand of the potter (Isa. 64:8; Jer. 18:1ff; Rom. 9:21). His counsel and his good pleasure is the final explanation of everything that happens or is allowed to happen. Read the Scriptures that describe him in this way (Ps. 33:11; Prov. 19:21; Isa. 46:10; Matt. 11:26; Acts 2:23; 4:28; Eph. 1:5, 9, 11). He does everything for his name's sake, and for his praise (Deut. 32:27; Jos. 7:9; I Sam. 12:22; Ps. 25:11; 31:3; 79:9; 106:8; 109:21; 143:11; Prov. 16:4; Isa. 48:9; Jer. 14:7, 21; Ezek. 20:9, 14, 22, 44). He needs nothing; he is all-sufficient (Job 22:2, 3; Ps. 50:18ff; Acts 17:25). He has life in himself (John. 5:26). He is the first and the last (Isa. 41:4; 44:6; 48:12; Rev. 1:8).

What does it mean to us that God is totally self-sufficient? It means that we must see how amazing is his purpose and his

love. If God does not need us it is all the more amazing that his
commitment to us is so great. God could have got on quite well
without us. So then why did he make us? This is a mysterious
question. Who can answer it? But part of the answer must be:
because he wanted to! Our very existence arises out of the fact
that God wanted someone to exist as well as himself. He made
millions of replicas of himself – the human race, millions of
people made in his image. We are not gods, but we are designed
and made to be companions of God. It is the most staggering
thing, something that we can scarcely get our minds round. We
are made to be the living companions of God! He could have got
on well without us but decided he wanted to share his love,
share his existence. He did not make just things, but living
creatures in his image, beings with minds and purposes and
wills of their own. In so doing he left open the possibility –
perhaps even probability or certainty, I do not know – that we
should rebel. He sent his Son to win us back, and to lead us in
such a way that it is our own voluntary love for him to fulfils
everything he planned for us at the beginning.

The independent God did not need us but wanted men and
women alongside him who would live and move and have their
being in himself.

We need to accept him the way he is and in the way in which
he acts. God is independent in himself, but also in his mind
(Rom. 11:34, 35), in his will (Dan. 4:35; Rom. 9:19; Eph. 1:5; Rev.
4:11), in his counsel (Ps. 33:11; Isa. 46:10), in his love (Hos. 14:5),
and in his power (Ps. 115:3). His view of reality is the right one.
His word tells us the way things are! It is no good disputing with
him. His plans are far beyond our understanding. Happiness
comes in accepting God as he is, and discovering him and the
goodness and faithfulness of his ways until we come to delight
in him. We submit to the mystery of his ways. We accept his
word. We ask him to be our father, our teacher, our guide, our
source of strength, our everything. He is independent of us, so
he is a fixed point of reference outside of us.

If God is the all-sufficient sovereign king of the universe and
yet invites us to be his companions, we must find the source, the
strength, the goal of our life in him. He is the source of all life
and existence. He is the fountain of all blessings. With him is the

fountain of life. In his life we find liveliness. In his light we find illumination.

God can be known as a fountain of life. Ask and it shall be given to you. Then get even more eager. Search and you will find. Then get more eager still. Knock persistently at the door of heaven. Hammer at the door and it will be opened. Say 'I will not let you go till you bless me'. God wants to be wanted. When we seek him with all our hearts, we find him.

There is another side to the coin in this matter. Although God is independent of us, God resembles human beings in many ways. God is human-like. God is personal. This is a fourth aspect of these basic characteristics of God, which I mention now after his spirituality, his oneness, and his independence.

God is 'he' not 'it', He has mind, will, feelings. The doctrine of the impassibility of God – the idea that God cannot suffer – is dubious.

Person is not a word that appears in the Bible to describe God. But it is a word (like Trinity and many other words) that we may use to summarize what the Bible says about God.

Actually God is often described as though he were an ordinary human person! God is often communicated to us in very human language. The Bible often talks of God as though he had a body. This language is not literal but it does show that there is something in God that corresponds to human nature. The Bible speaks of God's face (Gen. 4:14; 32:30; Exod. 33:11; Num. 6:25; Deut. 5:4; Ps. 27:8–9; Mic. 3:4; Matt. 18:10; I Cor. 13:12), God's eyes (Deut. 11:12; I Ki. 8:29; Ps. 11:4; I Pet. 3:12), God's ears (2 Ki. 19:16; Isa. 59:1; James 5:4), God's mouth (Num. 12:8; Isa. 1:20; Matt. 4:4), God's nose (Exod. 15:8; 2 Sam. 22:9, 16; Ps. 18:15), God's lips and tongue (Isa. 30:27; Job 11:5), God's arms (Exod. 6:6; Deut. 4:34; 5:15; 33:27; Isa. 52:10; Job 40:9; Luke 1:51), God's hands (Exod. 9:3; 13:9; Num. 11:23; Deut. 7:8; Ps. 89:13; Isa. 59:1; John 10:29; Acts 4:30; Rom. 10:21; Heb. 1:10; 10:31), God's feet (Ps. 2:11–12; 99:5; 132:7; Isa. 66:1; Matt. 5:35; I Cor. 15:25, 27), God's heart (Gen. 6:6; 8:21; I Sam. 2:35; Acts 13:22), God's voice (Gen. 3:8; Deut. 4:33; 5:25; Josh. 24:24; 1 Sam. 15:22; Ps. 29:3–5; Ezek. 10:5; Job 40:9; Mark 1:11; 9:7; John 12:28).

Then the Bible often talks of God as though he had human feelings and emotions. The Bible says that God is able to love

(Deut. 7:8; 10:15; Hos. 11:1; Isa. 43:4; John 3:16, 35; 2 Cor. 9:7; I John 4:9–10, 16), to repent (Gen. 6:6–7; Num. 23:19; I Sam. 15:11, 35; Jer. 4:28; Heb. 7:21), to have no pleasure in (Isa. 1:11; 65:12; Heb. 10:6, 10, 38), to laugh (Ps. 2:4; 5:8; 37:13), to be glad or to rejoice (Deut. 28:63; 30:9; Luke 15:7, 10), to be jealous (Exod. 20:5; 34:14), to be angry or wrathful (Exod. 4:14; Num. 11:10; Deut. 6:15; Judg. 2:14; Isa. 5:25; Jer. 4:8; Rom. 1:18; 9:22), to hate (Lev. 26:30; Amos 5:21), to be merciful (Exod. 34:6; Deut. 4:31; Ps. 103:8; Hos. 1:6–7; Jonah 4:2; Neh. 9:17, 31; Rom. 9:15–16; Phil. 2:27) and to have compassion (Deut. 13:17; 30:3; 2 Ki. 13:23; Ps. 86:15; Jer. 12:15; Rom. 9:15).

Then the Bible often talks of God as though he performs human actions. He sees (Gen. 16:13, 31; 31:42; Exod. 3:4; Matt. 6:4, 6, 18), hears (2 Sam. 22:7; I Ki. 8:30; John 11:41–42), speaks (Gen. 8:15; 46:2; Exod. 7:8; Num. 12:4; Isa. 8:11; Mark 12:26; Acts 18:9), whistles (Isa. 5:26; 7:18), rests and is refreshed (Gen. 2:2–3; Exod. 31:17), descends (Gen. 11:5, 7), takes in the way things smell (Gen. 8:21), walks or strolls (Gen. 3:8), and sits on his throne (Rev. 4:2; 5:1). These ways of speaking about God shows us that God resembles man (or better: man resembles God). He is 'He', not 'it'.

Why is God described in such an amazingly human way? The truth is God and man are much closer than is often realized. Sometimes God is described by Christians in a way that makes him too distant, and man is described in ways that make him too much of a nonentity. It is worth noting that God is never described as being like sinful man; he is not like man in wickedness. 'God is not man, that he should lie' (Num. 23:29). God is described in a human way because there is a closeness to God and man. Man is the image of God. But this truth can be put in another way. The same truth put another way round is that there are things in God that correspond to things in man. There is something in God that corresponds to our face, our eyes, our ears, and so on.

But there is surely another reason for this very human way of talking about God. It prepared the way for the coming of Jesus. It was not very unnatural for 'the Word', the eternal Son of God, to become man. It was already true that there was something about God that corresponds to a human being. God already was very human! It was only a small step further when God became man in Jesus Christ.

This is all very encouraging to us. It makes us know why it is so very easy for God to be sympathetic to us.

EIGHTEEN

The God whose Purpose does not Change

A fifth aspect of these basic characteristics of God is the description of God in the Bible as the unchanging God. This is an aspect of God's character that can easily be badly expressed. It has often been said – and I think rightly – that early Christian teaching picked up a few Greek philosophical ideas about God. One of them was the idea that God was static and coldly unchanging and without possibility of change or development. That is not the right way of thinking about the matter at all.

So as we come now to think about God's unchangeability or unchanging character we must be clear that by unchanging character I do not mean that God has no feelings. Some people are very apathetic and indifferent. No matter what happens they do not change. I do not mean anything like that! God does have feelings. There is the anger of God, and the compassion of God. He watches us and feels for us. 'God heard their groaning', says Exodus, 'God saw the people . . . God knew their condition' (Exod. 2:24–25). Equally Jesus – the mirror-image of God, the Father – had deep feelings. He could break down and weep at the tomb of Lazarus (John 11:35).

By unchanging character I do not mean that God does not have a story. Things happen in the life of God. God created. God sent Jesus. Judgment Day is coming. God is not like an endless swinging pendulum, always moving but never making progress. Even less is the God of the Bible a statue or a slab of concrete, a stationary God who never moves at all.

By God's unchanging character I do not mean that God is

unaffected by us. God responds to us. He takes notice of our prayers. He watches our sins. He is affected by our repentance. He rewards our obedience.

What I mean is that God's life does not change; he remains the same in his energy and in his existence as the living God. God's character does not change. God's promises do not change. The same promises of salvation remain on offer from generation to generation. In the depth of his being God is the one who redeems by the blood of the lamb, and he is not planning to change.[1]

God's habits stay the same. Most people have habits. I get up at roughly the same time every day (not very early!) and go to bed at the same time of day (late!). Mid-morning I have a cup of tea. I can always be found at my desk between certain hours in the morning. When in any kind of discussion I always proceed in a certain logical kind of order. And it can be guaranteed that every chapter of every book I write has a certain quantity of numbered points! Every bit of planning I do has a cast-iron backbone to it which I do not surrender lightly. But everything around the backbone is flexible and can be arranged moment by moment. And I preach in the same way! I have habits; so do you!

But God has habits as well, and they do not change! What are God's habits? His ways stay the same and we have to get to know them (Heb. 3:10). He has a habit of hating sin. He loves us to trust him. He has a habit of testing our obedience and our trust of him. He has a habit of allowing his promises to be delayed. And then he waits to see whether we will panic in unbelief and hostility. Then he comes to our rescue at the last moment. It is one of God's habits, and they do not change. He is habitually faithful. He habitually will not tolerate sin lightly. He will endure it, but he is not approving of it. There is no darkness in him at all, and we can never get him to approve of anything wicked.

God's purposes remain the same. To me, this is the most encouraging aspect of all, among the various aspects of God's unchangeableness. In Malachi 3:6 God says, 'I the LORD do not change; therefore you, O people of Jacob, are not consumed'. In the setting of Malachi it refers to God's determination to continue his purpose with Israel.

It is interesting and important that Malachi uses the term 'you people of Jacob'. We remember Jacob. He was born grabbing his brother's heel. There was nothing wicked about that except that it was rather symbolical of the way Jacob was all of his life. He was by nature a grabber. They gave him the name 'Jacob' which means something like 'One who grabs the heel'. He was a grabber by name, and grabber by nature. The early part of his life continued in much the same way as he had been born. He tricked Esau his brother out of his birthright. He tricked his father Isaac into giving the birthright to him. By nature he was a scheming, crafty fellow. Yet God had chosen him. 'Jacob have I loved', said God. God had a purpose to use Jacob. Through him and his twelve sons the people of Israel would come into being. Through his family Jesus would be born.

God was determined to use Jacob, and gave a promise before he was born or had done anything good or bad that God had plans to use him. As Jacob grew up it became apparent that Jacob was not a very nice person! Yet God had chosen him.

Centuries later Malachi is writing his prophecy. 'I the LORD do not change; therefore you, O people of Jacob, are not consumed'. One only has to read through the book of Malachi to see that the people were in a badly deteriorated spiritual condition. They had just been asking the question 'Where is the God of justice?' But if the God of justice were to act in exclusive justice, where would they stand? When God comes he comes as a refining fire! Do they really want God to act in total justice?

If anything, God might be thought likely to consume them altogether. But no! 'I the LORD do not change; therefore you, O people of Jacob, are not consumed'. This is the most comforting thought imaginable. I change. I have my ups and downs. If God's work in my life were to depend on me I would get nowhere. If God were to act in total justice and nothing but justice I would be consumed. But I need not fear. God is unchanging. He started a work in me – ignoring my weaknesses and my wickednesses. He sent Jesus to die for me on the cross. He sent his Spirit to open my eyes. He drew me into his plan. And now his purposes stay the same. He has a purpose for my life. No weakness of mine is likely to abort it. I am not consumed because he is determined to continue ever faithful to me. His commitment to me stays the same.

In some ways it is easier to lean on God's grace when we are young Christians than when we have been saved for a long time. When we are young in the LORD we know that we have just been rescued from ignorance and darkness. We know that the LORD has passed over all of our sins. He has said to us by his Spirit, 'Your sins are forgiven'. But when we get older in the LORD we sometimes feel that maybe things have now changed. We say to ourselves, 'I have been a Christian a long time now, and I haven't made the progress I would have liked. I am not what I used to be a long time ago, but I do not seem to be everything that I hoped to be either'. We feel guilty and ashamed that we have made so little progress.

It is at this point that we need Malachi's message. 'I the LORD do not change; therefore you, O people of Jacob, are not consumed'. The LORD has not changed towards us. He is as gracious to us now as he was when we were first saved. He knew the worst thing there was to know about us when he first saved us. Our weaknesses and wayward ways do not catch him by surprise. He does not say to us, 'You ought to be ashamed of yourself. I think I will give up on you'. No. God has not changed. He will never leave us or forsake us. Perhaps we are slow to grow, slow to learn. Actually our spiritual growth would speed up a little – or maybe a lot – if we really believe this. He does not give up on us. He is very determined to work out his purpose in us. We may as well get moving in cooperating with him.

His oath does not change. There are certain verses of the Bible that say God may change his mind (Gen. 6:6–7; 1 Sam. 15:11; 2 Sam. 24:15; Jonah 3:10; Joel 2:13–14). Those verses all deal with a situation where God has done something or given a promise or a threat – but then has left the situation open! There are other verses that say it is impossible for God to change his mind. 'The LORD has sworn and will not repent . . .' (Ps. 110:4)

The difference between the two types of verse is that in the first situation something is on offer or is being threatened. An open-ended promise or threat may not get fulfilled. The second set of Scriptures deal with an oath, and when an oath is taken the offer or threat is closed down. After the oath no change can take place. An oath of God cannot be turned aside. Jesus will not stop interceding. Why not? Because 'the LORD has sworn and will not change his mind' (Ps. 110:4). Despite David's sin with Bathsheda God's promise that the Saviour would be the seed of David could not be turned aside. Why not? Because God said, 'I have sworn to David' (Ps. 89:4); 'I will not violate my covenant or alter the word that went forth from my lips . . . His line will endure . . .' (Ps. 89:34, 35). God's oath cannot be changed. If you ever so please God that he takes an oath and says, 'I swear . . . I will indeed bless you . . .', then that blessing cannot be lost. The oath of God is unchangeable.

God's steadfast reliability is experienced in Jesus. God has already sworn that all of the 'seed of Abraham' shall be given to him. This is the anchor of our soul. Jesus is the same yesterday, today and for ever (Heb. 13:8). He is already in heaven. He is an anchor who has gone out of sight into heaven. We are tied to him. He is utterly faithful. He will save us to the uttermost point of glory (Heb, 7:25). We shall always find him to be the way He was when we found him at first. God does not change his purpose; we shall never be consumed.

Endnotes

1. The three points of this paragraph (life, character, promises) are developed by Packer J. I., *Knowing God* (Hodder, 1975), ch. 7. Since I do not wish to cover precisely the same ground, I leave these points undeveloped. Packer's work is recommended.

NINETEEN
The Power of the Living God

We are looking at some characteristics of God that I feel are more foundational than others, his very basic characteristics. It includes such things as God's spirituality, God's oneness, God's independence, his personality, his unchanging character, and so on.

We come now to think of the power of God. A good starting point is Jeremiah 32. Jeremiah was in an impossibly difficult position. It was the time of the Babylonian invasion. Jeremiah's preaching was getting him into trouble and he was in the private prison of the king (32:2). Then God comes to him and tells him that his nephew is on the way to ask Jeremiah to buy a field (32:6–7). It happens as he was told; the nephew arrives (32:8). But this field is in territory occupied by the Babylonians. What is the use of buying a field in occupied territory? And yet Jeremiah has been preaching that the people will be exiled to Babylon only temporarily and that one day his family will be back from exile and occupying their family-land once again. But at this point Jeremiah is puzzled. How can this field ever belong to his family? What is the point of buying it? At the moment the land is outside Jerusalem, and the Babylonian armies are out there. Jeremiah tells his puzzlement to God (32:17). As he prays he is meditating on the power of God.

Before we consider the details it is worth noticing how Jeremiah's view of God's character had an impact upon him in a very practical way. What could be more practical a matter than buying a field for one's later family to use? It does not seem a very theological matter. And yet if Babylonians are occupying your family-property it may be a very practical matter to know whether you do or do not believe in the power of God. Jeremiah certainly does believe in God's power.

Jeremiah's meditation on God's power begins with God's power in creation. He is very deeply moved at the thought of God's power. 'Ah, sovereign Yahweh!' he says (Jer. 32:17). It is a cry of emotion: 'Ah!' Jeremiah is not simply a theologian meditating in his study – as I am at this very moment. He is not in a study but in a dungeon! Whether God has power or not means a great deal to him at this time. 'Behold, you made the heavens and the earth by your great power and by your out-stretched arm . . .'.

Creation helps us to understand the power of God. God does not need anything to work on. When God created the heavens and the earth, 'in the beginning' (Gen. 1:1), there was nothing else existing other than himself. It was 'the beginning' of every-thing. God did not need to use any other material in order to bring about the marvels and the wonders of this creation in which we live.

The fact that this world is God's creation means that every circumstance and situation is accessible to him. God has power over every part of this creation because he is the one who made it in the first place. He has intimate familiarity with all of its workings. 'By the word of the LORD were the heavens made and all the parts of them by the breath of his mouth' (Ps. 33:6–7; see also Isa. 40:12. Ps. 107:25–30; Matt. 8:24–26). I like the way the Bible never says that 'it rains'. It says 'God sends rain'. It does not say 'The sun shines'; it says 'God makes the sun to shine' (Matt. 5:45).

God has power in caring for the history of the world. As Jeremiah sits in his dungeon, he is forced to think about the future. He is being invited to buy some land, but would his family ever have the use of it? He himself has been preaching that the nation is just about to be exiled to Babylon. Yet he has also been preaching that the exile will only last 70 years and then they will come back again. It is easy to believe that they will be exiled because the Babylonians are camping outside the city walls. Yet to believe that in 70 years Jeremiah's family will come back again takes great faith. Yet Jeremiah knows that God has power over the circumstances of the world, over history, over his family and its future. 'There is nothing too hard for you'.

God has power in his dealings with people. It is people who are involved in this situation. God has power over the Babylonians. God will give the city to the Babylonians (Jer. 32:27–29). But then he will bring Israel back (Jer. 32:37–41)! God has power over the hearts of people. Pharaoh swore he would not let Israel go (Exod. 5:2) but he did (Exod. 12:30, 31). The Pharisees promised themselves Jesus would not die at Passover time – but he did (Matt. 26:5). God rules over kings and presidents (Prov. 8:15, 16; Dan. 4:30–37).

God has power over the future. The promise is that 70 years later Israel will be restored to her territory again.

God has power over Satan. Who is behind this Babylonian conqueror? Satan. But God controls Satan (Job 1:10, 12; 2:6; Luke 22:31, 32). Satan has no power over God's children.

God has power in redemption. 'Ah, sovereign Yahweh!' he says, using the name which means 'The God who redeems by the blood of the lamb'. God is sovereignly powerful in saving and keeping his people. Think of how God saved Saul of Tarsus. He was breathing out threats and slaughter when God stepped into his life and turned him round (Acts 9:3–6). Think of the Philippian jailer (Acts 16:30–34). How quickly God can save and change a person's life!

God has power to keep us from falling. The people in Jeremiah 32 had sinned badly (as Jer. 32:30–35 suggests). Can God keep such a people? Yes! 'I will make an everlasting covenant. . . . I will not draw back from them. . . . I will put a fear of me in their hearts such that they will not turn away from me'. God is able to keep us from falling and to present us before the Father (Jude 24).

Jeremiah was being asked to live on this power of God. He was struggling with the thought of what he had done in buying his plot of land. He could scarcely believe it was possible for God to bring his family ever to make use of it. But he takes his problem to God. He asks God, God is this really what you are going to do? Can you really do it? God replies to Jeremiah, and echoes the very thing that Jeremiah said (Jer. 32:27). 'Nothing is too difficult for me'.

Another basic characteristic of God is that God is called the living God. The phrase 'as the Lord lives' occurs 43 times in the Old Testament. God says 'as I live' 23 times. The phrase 'the living God' occurs 14 times in the New Testament (as in Heb. 9:14), and the 'living Father' occurs in John 6:57. Jesus is said to be the 'Son of the living God' (Matt. 16:16). When the Bible calls God 'the living God' it is referring to the way in which God is so active and powerful. He participates in our lives. He has a habit of intervening (although of course he is present all the time as well!).

Our view of God must not be cold or static. God is not just an idea or a philosophy. He is active and alive. This is one of the differences between God and the idols. (Jer. 10:6–20; I Ki. 18:27; I Thess. 1:9).

a. Our God is full of surprises. It is not a matter of routine to know him. Meetings are not a matter of routine. Think of the meeting in Acts 20:7–12. It was full of surprises. We may expect interventions. It was the 'living God' who saved Daniel from the lions (Dan. 6:19–27). It was the 'living God' who helped David (I Sam. 17:26, 36; see also 2 Ki. 19:4; Deut. 5:26; Ps. 84:2).

b. Our God is a God who gives life or liveliness. Think of what Jesus said to the woman at the well. He promises 'living water', eternal life springing up within us (see also 2 Cor. 3:6; John 6:51; 7:37–39). God is a fountain of life (see John 3:16; Ps. 36:9; John 4:10).

c. God responds to us. Think of the story in 1 Kings 18. The prophets of Baal prayed to dead idols. Elijah swore, 'As Yahweh is alive . . .', and prayed to the living God. 'The God who answers by fire, let him be God!'. God responds to us. He responds to our praying.

He responds to our sins. It is a fearful thing to fall into the hands of the living God (Heb. 10:31).

He responds to our obedience. Those who honour him, he honours. Those who despise him, he despises (1 Sam. 2:30). He takes note of how we regard him – because he is the living God.

TWENTY
How to Discover God

I have not finished my meditations on the doctrine of God. There is more to come, and I expect to write another little book about God. We must think more of God's vastness, eternity, knowledge, wisdom, truthfulness, faithfulness, love, mercy, grace, patience, long-suffering, compassion, goodness, holiness, righteousness, anger, jealousy.

But for the moment let us end with this thought: God is meant to be known and discovered personally.

Let me put down a few hints to be guidelines to us in 'the pursuit of God' (as A.W. Tozer's great book puts it).

1. Believe that God is there. God is real; God is alive. We are worshipping the living God. Believe that God is there. Hebrews 11:6 says, 'Without faith it is impossible to please God'. It goes on to tell us what sort of faith the writer is thinking about. 'He who comes to God must believe that God is there'. God is there! Sometimes God is so real to us that we seem to be almost feeling him. His presence can be so real, it is almost a physical experience. But a lot of the time it is not like that at all! By faith, believe that God is there.

2. Believe that God is close. God is not a long way away. He is not simply some creator who is a million miles above the sky. It is not like making a long-distance call on the telephone to some far-off country, where you have to shout down the line to get heard! No it is more like sitting with a friend on a sofa made for two! God is right there beside you. In him we live and move and have our being. He gives us life. He gives us breath. He keeps our lungs moving.

3. Believe that God is willing to speak. We serve a living God.

He is there and he is not silent. God likes to speak. He has been speaking ever since he existed, talking to his Son, talking to his Spirit. Then he created men and women to have more people to talk to. He would visit them in the cool of the day just to talk to them (Gen. 3:8). God likes talking. He is willing to talk to you.

God talks to us about big things and little things. He will reveal to us what his Word means. It is possible to be taught the meaning of the Word by the working of the Spirit in our heart. God himself is willing to take the words of Scripture and speak them again in such a way that we know what they mean. We can feel it! We know it is true. I know this is a teaching that can easily be abused, but nevertheless it is a fact that everyone who knows God's truth does so because of his experience of the Holy Spirit.

God talks to us about little things as well as big things. Not long ago, I got lost in Dar-Es-Salaam, capital-city of Tanzania. I asked God to rescue me, and he told me to stay exactly where I was. I was sitting in a café at the time, so I stayed there, doing nothing and hoping the waiters were not wondering why I was sitting there so long. An hour later God said to me, 'Now go outside and start trying to find your way'. I walked outside the café and stood there on the roadside wondering what I should do next. I began to walk over the road where I could see some Tanzanian policemen who I thought might help me. I was just about to speak to them when suddenly someone walked by and smiled at me! For a second or two I could not think who he was but then I remembered. He was a man who had once interpreted for me when I was preaching in Tanzania. So I stopped him. 'Brother, don't go! I need your help!'. Within a few minutes he was taking me to where I needed to go. If I had walked out of that café five minutes earlier or five minutes later, I would have missed him.

God talks to us about little things as well as big things. He will help us find lost keys or lost friends. He will help us in a quarrel. He will whisper into our hearts exactly what to do, to say, exactly where to go. He gives us a lot of freedom, but when we need him, he will talk to us.

4.   Believe that God may be approached by the blood of Jesus Christ. We do not come to God because we are worthy. Personally

I have often found that it is when I am least worthy that God is most gracious, most willing to speak, most willing to act on my behalf.

I have often wondered why it is that sometimes when we are at our worst, God is so kind to us. I think it is because much of the time we are trusting in how good we are. But when we are at our worst, when we feel bad, it almost forces us to plead nothing but the blood of Jesus Christ. We go to God, and we say to him 'Lord I feel bad at the moment, but I am just asking you to be with me because of the blood of Jesus'. 'Lord, Jesus died for me! Lord, Jesus took that sin away on the cross!' 'Lord, don't look at my weakness. Lord, please look at the blood of Jesus, and hear me'. I find that God is very moved when we plead the blood of his Son.

5. Do not be afraid of God. I know God is fearsome and awe-inspiring. He is a consuming fire. And yet the Bible tells us to approach him boldly. Trust that God's plans for you are good. What holds most of us back from discovering God is that most of the time we are afraid of God in a wrong way. The Bible does speak of the fear of God. The fear of God is a matter of knowing how seriously he hates sin and how searching is his judgment. Yet at the same time we must know that there is no reason to think God is a vindictive tyrant or that he is against us. It is the devil who paints a picture of God that is intended to frighten us away. Think of God as one who wishes to be the greatest kind of father that you ever could imagine. A true father, one who truly wishes to care for you, protect you, guide you. . . .

6. Surrender yourself to him. Tell God, through Jesus, that you want to utterly trust him, utterly give your life to him. In the Old Testament people would offer 'whole burnt offerings'. They would take an animal and sacrifice it entirely and utterly. The Bible tells Christians – people who are trusting the blood of Jesus Christ – to give themselves totally and utterly to God. It is not something that we should be afraid of. When we give ourselves totally to God in the name of Jesus we discover that God's will is reasonable, good, acceptable, perfect. God's plans and desires for us are wholly good. When we truly discover God's will for our lives we shall find out that it is greater than anything we could have planned for ourselves. It leads to happiness.

7. Consult him frequently. God is a friend. He likes to be consulted. He likes us to share what is happening, and get his advice and leading. Often in the stories of the Bible we are told that someone 'enquired of the Lord' (e.g. 1 Sam. 23:1–5; 2 Sam. 2:1). David would ask God for confirmation before he went into battle. When David forgot to consult God he made major mistakes. God likes to be consulted. It is part of what friendship means. And God tends not to reveal things to us if we do not seek his revelations.

8. Understand his dealings with you. Sometimes strange events seem to come into our lives. They are so unusual we feel that God must be doing something special. In Genesis 25:22 Rebekah was conscious of something unusual happening within her womb, and an unusual event calls for an unusual enquiry. She asks God about it (Gen. 25:22) and she gets an answer. The two children are to become forefathers of two nations (25:23). Rebekah was given a special revelation as a result of enquiry when she felt God was doing something unusual.

9. I have mentioned already the need to spend time with God. Find a way. Make a programme. But give God time.

10. Genuinely live for his glory. The glory of God is the radiation of his character. To live for the glory of God is to live genuinely wanting the greatness of God to be seen. Few of us live this way. There is nothing that would take us out of ourselves, nor that would produce sheer kindness and love in us, nothing that would lead us into meekness more than to have it as our desire that the greatness of God's character will be seen for what it is.

Live this way. Start with the cleansing blood of Jesus Christ. Walk in the light. Make confession of sins a daily habit. God is real; God is alive. God is close, and willing to speak. Approach him boldly. Surrender yourself to him. Consult him. Seek him. Spend time with him.

And you will discover God!

Enjoying God's Worldwide Church
Michael Eaton

- Is 'Church' necessary?
- What is the Church?
- How do I enjoy the Church?

Michael Eaton encourages the reader to look at the Church from a worldwide perspective, in order to 'enlarge our vision'. He also shows how we, as individuals, fit into God's overall plan and purpose in the Church.

As the author says, 'To see the purpose of God for his whole people will stop us from being small-minded, and perhaps open to us things that God is doing that may not have reached our own local congregation . . .'

'A world-class scholar and writer, Dr Michael Eaton is really tomorrow's theologian . . . Thoroughly biblical and historically sensitive, what he writes is put simply and plainly in a way that appeals to the youngest Christian and yet challenges the most sophisticated thinker . . . I predict that he will be the talk of tomorrow's generation.'
R.T. Kendall, Westminster Chapel.

1-85078-321-7

OM
publishing

Living a Godly Life
Michael Eaton

- What is holiness?
- Why should we be holy?
- When does sanctification take place?
- Who does the sanctifying?

Michael Eaton answers these questions simply and clearly in this straightforward presentation of the biblical teaching of sanctification. From this basis he moves on to provide basic principles as to how we can grow in holiness in our daily lives.

This book is an excellent starting place for those seeking to understand and communicate their faith.

'As Michael Eaton writes he wipes the dust off theology. From being intimidating it becomes an adventure . . . These books arrest the mind, capture the heart and empower the will.'
Ben Davies, Senior Pastor, Bracknell Family Church.

1-85078-308-x

OM
publishing